L. C. MATHER

B. Com (London) FCIS *Fellow of the Institute of Bankers*

THE
LENDING BANKER

A Review of the principles of Bank Lending
Unsecured Advances and Balance Sheets
and the Banker

WATERLOW (LONDON) LIMITED

By the same author

Banker and Customer Relationship and
The Accounts of Personal Customers (1957)
Fifth (Revised) Edition 1977

The Accounts of Limited Company Customers
Fourth (Revised) Edition 1978

Securities Acceptable to The Lending Banker
Third (Revised) Edition 1972

THE LENDING BANKER

First Edition 1955
Second Edition 1960
Third (Revised) Edition 1966
Fourth (Revised) Edition 1972
Fifth (Revised) Edition 1979

©
WATERLOW (LONDON) LIMITED
Holywell House
Worship Street
London EC2A 2EN
Printed in Great Britain by Waterlow (London) Limited
ISBN 0 900791 48 9

Preface to First Edition

Bank lending is an art as well as a science and, in addition to the wealth of technical and legal knowledge which is so essential in his business, the able branch manager by dint of experience has to acquire and develop the aptitude to assess every request for an advance according to innumerable factors appertaining to the potential borrower, his business, capital position and prospects in relation to current economic and financial conditions. A good banker learns by his own mistakes and by the experience of his forebears, and these articles, originally published in the Educational Section of *The Bankers' Magazine*, were written in an attempt to produce a concise and clear picture of the general principles of bank lending regardless of the security which may be available. They are based on practice and embrace a field not hitherto covered completely by the standard banking text books. Originally written in response to many requests received whilst lecturing for the Institute of Bankers throughout the country, this demand for a reprint of the articles affords ample evidence of the need to fill a gap in banking literature. If the contents prove helpful to those in the vast banking business who cannot by force of circumstances hope to gain wide experience before undertaking the responsibility of branch management, my labours will not have been in vain.

For obvious reasons, the contents are limited to general principles and, as the busy banker cannot spare the time to become a specialist expert in balance sheets and accountancy problems, the whole picture is presented in the simplest possible manner limiting the review to the bare essentials. The object is to be helpful to the practical lender and no attempt has been made to educate the technical student. A really detailed analysis of a customer's balance sheet and profit and loss figures is usually beyond the function or requirements of the branch banker, but he must be able to assess the position at a glance, raise pertinent questions on points of weakness, and reach a logical conclusion as a guide to the final decision. It is the aim of this little book to assist the reader to that extent only.

The method of approach and general scheme of the contents are self-explanatory, but in conclusion I wish to pay tribute to those innumerable practical banking chiefs, colleagues and friends of wide experience who have unwittingly helped by their daily guidance and encouragement in the production of this volume. I can only hope that the printed words will prove to be of similar assistance to readers who look forward to assuming the responsibilities of branch management in their bank in the future.

RIVERHEAD
KENT.   L.C.M.
August, 1955.

Preface to the Fifth Edition

The demand for this practical guide to the lending banker continues apace and a fresh edition has now been prepared by Mr. T. E. H. Crawford, Assistant General Manager of Midland Bank Limited, who was good enough to edit the fourth edition.

We live in a rapidly changing world when it is thought necessary to protect the consumer or borrower regardless of the efficiency and understanding of the lender and of the cost entailed in introducing endless complicated and utterly impracticable legislative measures. All these fresh complications have been brought into this new edition and I am indebted to Mr. Crawford for the way in which he has devoted himself to amending the text where necessary to bring it all completely up-to-date. I warmly acknowledge his expert help, without which it would have been impossible to produce this fresh edition.

SEAL
KENT,   L.C.M.
January, 1979.

Chapter I

The Basic Function of a Bank as a Lender

Before considering the basic principles of bank lending it is well to establish at the outset that the prime function of a clearing bank as a lender in this country today is to afford short-term accommodation when required for approved purposes. This may appear to be a sweeping assertion in view of the diversification of clearing bank activities following the changes in banking practice after the introduction in October 1971 of new regulations for financial institutions, now known simply as "Competition and Credit Control"—the title of the Bank of England memorandum outlining the new procedures.

One of the most important features of this new financial environment is the active participation of the clearing banks in the London money markets. Using their extensive branch networks the banks acquire funds ranging in term from overnight to periods of a few years as well as negotiate direct employing specialist central departments or subsidiaries with companies, public sector bodies and other financial concerns. Their primary aim in these activities is not that of the dealer in money but essentially to protect the liquidity position of the bank and to provide term deposits to meet the growing demand for advances repayable in the medium or long term range. Although the principles of lending long are basically the same as lending short, medium-term and fixed loan facilities demand specialist skills and are outside the scope of this book which is primarily concerned with normal bank lending from the standpoint of a branch banker in a clearing bank.

COMPETITION AND CREDIT CONTROL

The new arrangements for regulating the banking system agreed between the clearing banks, other City banking institutions and the Bank of England in 1971 represented a fundamental change in the commercial practices of banks in the United Kingdom. Despite this widening of financial operations the axioms of bank management set out in this chapter hold true. In particular the bank must ensure that those funds which can be withdrawn by customers upon demand are employed in short-term lending and that sufficient liquidity is available to meet the bank's day-to-day requirements. The extension of clearing bank activities into fields previously considered the prerogative of the specialist lender emphasize rather than lessen the importance of the basic principles of sound lending set out below.

The quantitative controls employed by the Authorities for some years whereby fixed "ceilings" on total bank lending were imposed were abolished. The banks are free to lend and raise deposits, the demand for bank facilities being governed purely by the price of money. A common reserve asset ratio of 12½ per cent. replaced the previous 28 per cent. "liquidity ratio" and were applied to all banks; finance houses must maintain 10 per cent. of their deposits in reserve assets. These are closely defined, being basically balances at the Bank of England, money at call and short notice and certain acceptable paper such as gilt-edged securities with one year or less to maturity, Treasury Bills and a fixed proportion of certain commercial bills. An important exclusion is cash in tills and certain loans provided under the special schemes for export and ship-building finance.

All financial institutions quote independently for deposits of every type with fixed maturities or on notice of any length. Commercial banks' balance sheets contain an "hierarchy" of deposits ranging from those repayable on demand to fixed terms or to varying lengths of notice to withdraw by the depositor. As a direct consequence a bank's ability to lend at medium or long term is enhanced provided always that a balance is maintained between the maturity of the loans and the bank's commitment to meet depositors' withdrawals. Each bank now fixes its own base rate as a yardstick against which many lending and deposit interest rates are quoted. The relevance of the Bank of England's Minimum Lending Rate is clearly material but not in any way fixed. Theoretically these independent base rates can move to meet the market changes in the pattern of interest rates and the supply of and demand for money to and from the banking system. In practice banks keep their base rates at a very similar level. This lack of discrepancy in bank base rates has been the subject of criticism from public commentators, both private and political, suggesting this conformity indicates a failure to compete. The exact opposite is probably true, the few attempts by individual banks to stand out at different levels of interest rate to those prevailing for clearing bank funds have been shortlived. This tendency towards uniformity stems from the working of a free market with flows of funds moving quickly to compensate for irregular quotations forcing the offerer to move into line or the market to move to new levels.

Quotations for both deposits and advances use the individual bank base rates as a guiding star but inevitably an active and innovative market such as that prospering in London produces its own mechanisms; one of the more notable being the London Inter-bank Offer Rate or LIBOR. The use of this medium to describe the value of funds on offer in the market—quoted if necessary at a particular time—is one of these innovations provided to meet the demands of the participants, lender and borrower, and an essential feature of the basic flexibility of the City as a primary money market.

The new regulations represented a logical extension from the clearing banks' decision in February, 1970 to disclose "true" profit figures, waiving their rights under the Companies' Act 1948 to make undisclosed transfers to inner reserves. The pressure of a competitive market for money is upon bank profits which now bear a closer relationship to the relative ability and efficiency of the bank's management and staff. This implies a greater emphasis on the banker's capacity to lend safely and well and on his entrepreneurial flair in obtaining the best long term return on the funds entrusted to him.

THE BRANCH BANKER—A SHORT-TERM LENDER

The main source of the bank's funds, deposits held for personal and corporate customers to meet their transmission or short-term savings requirements, explains the care which has always to be given to the liquidity of advances. A clearing bank remains basically a short-term lender. The monthly statement issued by the London Clearing Banks in August, 1978 disclosed that the banks had lent £29,109 million, but their aggregate paid-up capital and published reserves were only a fraction of the total lent. Clearly, therefore, the banks are not lending their own money but furnish advances from the deposits which they receive from other customers. The deposits totalled £37,307 million, of which £15,841 million was held on current account repayable upon demand, and the major part of the balance on deposit, subject usually to seven days' notice of withdrawal. Thus the banks had lent 78·0 per cent. of their deposits. The deposits are all repayable by the bank upon demand or at very short notice from the customers. Most of the advances are also technically repayable by borrowers upon demand from the bank, but the speed with which they can actually be recovered must depend upon the ability of the borrower to obtain the cash from his own resources or from realisation of the security held, if any. From these simple statements of fact it is obvious that the banker cannot lend long any substantial proportion of funds which have been borrowed short from other customers. To tie-up money for lengthy periods would be to accept the risk of experiencing difficulty in meeting an unexpected demand for deposits.

The liquid position of our banks is unimpeachable and they remain completely free from any legal control in such respect. Relying on the experience of their forebears over many decades, banks today know how to use their assets to maximum advantage without impairing their ability at all times to meet demands from customers for cash withdrawals. To this end deposits are spread amongst assets with varying degrees of liquidity. Apart from monies locked-up in premises and investments in associated banks and subsidiaries in the United Kingdom and elsewhere, advances would normally be the most difficult asset to realise. Their total must

9

accordingly be kept within bounds and their quality and liquidity measured with care. On the other hand, if advances are allowed to fall too low the earning capacity of the banks will suffer, because, if sound, they are beyond doubt the banks' most lucrative source of income.

It is neither necessary nor opportune to explore further the distribution of the bank assets, but an independent study of the up-to-date balance sheet of any clearing bank will be helpful to those who are not conversant with the general trend.

FORMALISED PERSONAL LENDING SERVICES

Despite continuous Government constraint on bank lending for personal consumption, the expansion of consumer lending has widened and changed in application and purpose as the years go by. The development of Personal Loans in 1958 marked the beginning of this trend which has grown in momentum so that a separate chapter has been devoted to these services because they are a real test of the lending banker.

NON-STERLING LOANS

The widespread introduction of Government controls on capital expenditure outside national boundaries and the phenomenon of the deficit in overseas trade of the United States produced a flood of US dollars throughout the developed world and particularly in Europe. This imbalance in world finance provided an opportunity for a unique financial market, that of eurocurrencies which used initially dollar claims, held mainly by Europeans to finance the requirements of international trade and investment. The strength and scope of this market, with London as the main centre of its operation, has been clearly demonstrated despite many financial crises and the participation of the clearing banks has grown accordingly. The same basic principles of lending apply regardless of the form of currency used by the banker to make the advance, but special consideration needs to be given to the exigencies of the rates of exchange, the exchange control regulations imposed by the Bank of England and central banks abroad, withholding taxes in overseas countries, etc. The market has now expanded beyond the purely US dollar base to include loans and issues of bonds in most trading currencies. It is an important and useful adjunct to the London banker's financial armoury which needs prudent administration and specialist lending knowledge.

OTHER SOURCES OF FINANCE

1. *Capital*

It has been said that in any modern economy finance may be defined as the provision of money where and when it is required. The primary source of finance for any business must be from the proprietors, who presumably have the cash available to support their confidence in the trading prospects of the venture, or are able to attract capital from others in the market. Whether the amount required by a limited company can best be found by the issue of ordinary shares and/or preference shares (of which there are many varieties) and/or debenture stock, must depend upon the extent and precise nature of the needs and the risk entailed. The major risk is usually accepted by the ordinary shareholder, whilst the preference shareholder is content to accept a smaller reward in return for a degree of priority. The debenture holder, on the other hand, lends his money at a satisfactory rate usually against security and often subject to repayment at an agreed date. It may well be that the proprietors will prefer to borrow against debentures repayable from accumulated profits in instalments or wholly on a convenient date, rather than allow outside parties to obtain an interest in the business by the purchase of ordinary capital. Care may nevertheless be necessary in case borrowing long-term against the security of a debenture handicaps the ability of the company to borrow temporarily from its bankers for normal working capital. If a company proposes to issue debenture stock but still wishes to borrow occasionally from its bank, then the problem should be discussed fully with the bank before issue of the debenture. Arrangements can often be made to give the bank certain prior security for advances granted in the ordinary course of business up to a stated limit and available at any one time to prevent the operation of the Rule in Clayton's Case against the bank.

The type of capital required, the minimum terms upon which it should be issued to attract the market and the legal essentials involved are matters for the expert, and the proprietors should be recommended to approach an Issuing House either direct or through their brokers. Pending completion of arrangements for a fresh issue of capital or debenture stock by an established company, it may be that arrangements can be made to borrow from the company's banker. Such bridging of the gap between the outlay and the receipt of fresh capital is temporary finance within the function of a bank, but the bank will normally wish to be satisfied that arrangements are well advanced for the prospective capital issue before allowing any extensive overdraft. Otherwise repayment may prove to be long delayed. In recent years at least one clearing bank has established, in conjunction with a merchant bank, a specialist company to invest in enterprises likely to seek public quotation within a few years. The intention is to provide bank finance prior to a successful issue of shares when the bank is repaid hopefully with a capital profit.

However such capital may be raised, the general sound financial principle for any business unit is that its capital should be sufficient to cover the purchase of all its fixed assets and to leave a reasonable margin available for working capital. In this respect a fixed asset may be defined as any agent of production acquired to be retained in the business for such purpose. Within this class may usually be found all premises, machinery, fixtures and fittings, lorries, cars and loose tools not being goods produced by the business itself for sale to third parties. Current assets on the other hand are those purchased for cash out of working capital in order that they may, in due course, be turned with profit into cash again. Taking any cycle of production, raw materials are purchased and further cash paid in wages for labour expended on the raw material to turn it, with sundry other on-costs, into the finished product held as stock until sold and then turned into debtors pending collection of the cash from them. Thus stocks on hand, work-in-progress, debtors and cash form the normal current assets of a unit, and working capital is required to carry them through the production cycle. In approved cases a bank can rightly furnish part of the working capital, but it is not its normal function to provide long-term advances for capital outlay. The small private company, particularly where controlled by family interests, may wish to avoid an approach to the market for fresh capital because control of the company may have to be given up in order to attract sufficient cash from the public. This natural anxiety of entrepreneurs to retain control of the business they have developed from small beginnings is understandable, but unless they can manage with mortgage finance on the lines set out below, or attract what they require by way of preference capital, with limited voting rights, or a debenture issue, with no power to the holders to intervene if the business remains in a healthy condition, they will have to face up to some loss of control or limit their expansion to what can be financed from profits retained in the business. The proprietors of this type of family company are nowadays often forced into the capital market in any event to provide for the heavy incidence of death duties payable on their interest in the company upon their death. From this aspect the benefits of family control or virtual sole ownership of any company are most limited, and the loss of control to outside interests may have tax advantages. In such cases expert legal and financial advice is essential.

2. *Mortgage finance*
Instead of obtaining fresh capital, a long-term requirement may be met by the mortgage of a property. This method of finance may be more attractive to the sole trader or partnership than to the larger limited company, but providing the borrower does not attempt a scheme with repayments beyond the capacity of income (and the lender will watch this) it is a prudent means of financing a capital purchase or of raising working capital against a fixed asset already acquired from capital.

The simplest example of such finance is that of the small householder who buys his property with the help of a building society. The borrower provides a reasonable equity or deposit at the outset from his capital and the society lends the balance, repayable usually in monthly instalments over a long period. The history of the building society movement, a peculiarly British institution, emphasises the social aspect of its objectives, to further owner occupation of private dwelling houses. Successive Governments have encouraged this desirable policy by granting special tax concessions to the societies, which help to deter banks from competition in this specialised field. Nevertheless, opportunities arise for worthwhile medium-term facilities, often in the more expensive properties usually beyond the mandate of the societies, where a bank can provide assistance to reputable borrowers within the confines of the bank's deposit structure. The opportunities afforded to the commercial banks by freer access to term deposits has enabled competitive facilities to be made to prospective house purchasers with 'special' problems—larger than average require-ments for mortgage loans or other unusual needs. The inroads made by building societies into the deposit and savings markets suggest more direct competition by the banks may take place, enabling house owners to improve or extend their properties at reasonable cost and providing the banker with a secure form of personal loan.

Industrial mortgages are outside the primary purpose of building societies and their capacity to provide funds for such needs is restricted. Large-scale mortgages may, however, be suitable business for an insurance company anxious to invest funds for long-term remunerative rates. There may be opportunities for bankers to provide medium-term funds for this purpose or "bridging finance" pending the arrangement of a mortgage to repay the bank debt which would be more suitable to the banker's short-term lending function.

For farmer customers needing long-term finance the Agricultural Mortgage Corporation Ltd. is available as a specialist lender against the security of a mortgage on farm land. In its trading year to March, 1978, this Corporation lent over £46 million against fresh mortgage loans, whilst advances of more than a further £15·7 million were approved by the directors subject to completion of the legal formalities. Total loans outstanding at March, 1978 were more than £338 million advanced against the security of first mortgages of agricultural land, farmhouses and buildings. To finance these loans the Corporation had capital and reserves of about £13·7 million, plus secured loan capital of £325 million, consisting of long-term debentures of £282 million and short bonds of £29 million and £14 million borrowed from the Ministry of Agriculture, Fisheries and Food. In short, it has lent its own funds long against full security. Commercial banks provide a wider range of facilities to support the agricultural industry and to reduce the need for food imports; special loans are marketed for machinery and fertilisers, to extend or modernise farm buildings as well as medium-term mortgages. A considerable expertise has been acquired in providing specially-designed financial assistance to the experienced farmer of proved ability. These loans have proved profitable and safe—compared with lending to many major industries in the United Kingdom in the last twenty years agriculture has a fine record of progress and stability.

3. Other specialist long-term lenders
Finance for Industry Limited

Finance for Industry Limited is a private institution owned by the English and Scottish clearing banks (85 per cent.) and the Bank of England (15 per cent.). It acts as a holding company for its principal subsidiaries, Industrial and Commercial Finance Corporation Limited (I.C.F.C.), Finance Corporation for Industry Limited (F.C.I.) and Finance for Shipping Limited (F.F.S.), and for other subsidiary companies involved in leasing, property and consultancy activities.

I.C.F.C. provides financial advice and long term finance for the smaller business in amounts ranging from £5,000 to £2 million. F.C.I. undertakes the provision of medium and long term finance at fixed or fluctuating rates for larger companies in amounts ranging from £1 million to £25 million. F.F.S. finances British shipowners and provides post-delivery finance for ships built in United Kingdom shipyards and acquires and owns ships which are chartered to responsible shipowners. The group is also concerned with the provision of industrial premises for small and medium-sized companies and provides a management consultancy service and training service for small companies.

At 31st March, 1978, F.F.I.'s commitment to British industry and commerce totalled £614 million with a further £104 million, held as liquid funds available for new investment. These were financed by shareholders' funds of £126 million and borrowings and other resources of £583 million. Under the arrangements made in response to the Governor of the Bank of England's initiative in November, 1974, the shareholders were committed to provide up to £85 million of additional share capital of which £25 million has been subscribed. This commitment will enable total borrowings to be increased to over £1,200 million, providing over £800 million for further investment, in addition to the return flow from existing investments which is being re-invested at a rate of over £50 million per annum.

In addition to the commitment to subscribe further share capital the shareholders have made available standby facilities of £100 million. The backing provided by these facilities has given F.F.I. access to all the borrowed funds it has needed to date for industrial investment and will provide continuing support for substantial levels of future demand. The Group's borrowings are not guaranteed by either the shareholders or the Government and F.F.I. has developed its own first class credit rating to obtain the funds it needs. These funds are provided mainly in the form of loan stocks listed on The Stock Exchange and subscribed both by the major financial institutions and by the private investor.

A further direct channel has recently been added to enable the small saver to invest in British industry. F.F.I. now accepts fixed term deposits for periods of three to ten years which are allocated particularly to the small and medium-sized sector served by I.C.F.C. Whatever the conditions prevailing elsewhere, whether in the stock market, among the other institutions or in the economy at large, F.F.I. and its subsidiaries have never had to refuse applications for lack of funds.

4. *Industrial finance*

Hire purchase facilities are available for the acquisition of certain fixed assets, mainly motors, lorries and machinery, and to carry debtors by way of block discounting. Providing the hirer can service the debt comfortably from income within the term allowed, no difficulty arises, but the accommodation is often more costly than bank borrowing. The financial services provided by finance houses have grown in range and sophistication so that some overlap with banking facilities occurs. The difference in approach stems largely from the relatively limited access to funds, all interest-bearing, normally available to a finance house. It is interesting to note that most major finance houses have been acquired by clearing banks, since the first investments in this sector in 1958. These subsidiaries join other specialist companies in the banking groups involved in leasing machinery, vehicles or major assets such as ships and aircraft. They also provide factoring services accepting responsibility for the collection of amounts owed to a company and discounting a proportion of these in advance of receipt of the amount due.

The ability of banking groups to market combined facilities covering these specialist forms of direct assistance so that companies may obtain particular assets or fund a range of debts in addition to the "traditional" form of working capital overdraft has been a slowly emerging feature of modern banking.

5. *Internal finance*

Finally, it is well to note that a business can itself provide finance internally by the retention of profits and/or by the deferred payment of creditors. The prudent retention of profits to expand any business unit and to provide for a rainy day needs little explanation. It is something additional to provision for replacements by way of depreciation. But the use of cash resources otherwise needed to meet taxation, for example, may be dangerous if the cash cannot be replaced in time to meet the liability. Any attempt to employ in the business monies collected under PAYE principles or for purchase tax pending payment to the Inland Revenue is likewise dangerous. If money required for taxation or to meet other creditors is locked-up in new machinery or work-in-progress, it cannot always be replaced in time and the business may already have borrowed all it can from the bank to bolster a shortage of working capital. These aspects claim the due attention of the lending banker when analysing the balance sheet of a borrower.

As a last example of a lender with an entirely different function from that of a banker, it is well to mention the registered moneylender who employs his own funds and, in the normal course of his business, charges high rates for accommodation to cover the very heavy risk he readily accepts. This brief review of the alternative sources of finance gives a glimpse of the changing role of banks and banking groups as financiers for business enterprise. What began and still remains essentially as advances for short-term needs to bridge gaps or to provide day-to-day working funds has spread into a number of related fields. There remains the basic principles of liquidity for the banker to follow as well as the need to spread advances. It would clearly be unwise to lend unduly large amounts to a few borrowers, however strong they may appear to be. The danger of vulnerability in this respect is severely restricted by the refusal normally to furnish fixed capital.

Chapter II

The Basic Principles of Lending

It is possible to draw from experience certain basic principles of bank lending, but they are to be regarded essentially as statements of general tendencies only and not irrefutable laws inelastic and incapable of wider interpretation to meet given circumstances. They are perhaps akin to economic laws in that given certain facts and other things being equal a prescribed course should follow. They are neither independent nor unbreakable. These principles and their requirements are all closely interwoven and cannot be isolated, whilst in many instances the advantages supporting one or more principles may completely outweigh the weaknesses resulting from the failure of the proposal to meet the other principles. Thus an advance has often to be granted despite its failure to fulfil all the basic principles of good lending. The reader must accordingly approach this study with an elastic outlook, accepting the principles as a guide to perfection but recognising that in the practical competitive field risks have sometimes to be accepted and advances granted which fail to comply with many of the approved canons.

There are three basic principles behind all bank lending.

1. *Safety.*

Above all, the loan must be safe, which demands that it should be granted to a reliable borrower who can repay from reasonably sure sources within a relatively short period. The liquidity of the advance in the ordinary course of business should be unquestionable and the safety requirement should usually be supported by the deposit of approved security as an insurance against unforeseen developments. Very many features demand examination under this wide heading, but they all combine to enable the banker to decide whether the proposal is sound enough to afford sufficient safety for the advance.

2. *Suitability.*

The requirements of many borrowers may be completely free from all risks, but fail to comply with this second principle which stems from the banker's wish to concentrate his lending on purposes which are desirable from the standpoint of the economic health of the nation. It is no part of banking business to finance gambling or undue speculation or to provide long-term capital, and in past years consideration had also to be given to Government controls and directions in the efforts to combat inflation.

The purpose of the advance and its likely benefit, or otherwise, to the country is thus an important feature to be weighed in the balance.

3. *Profitability.*

For obvious reasons there is little point in a banker granting facilities which do not produce directly or indirectly some profit to the lender. In these days of ever increasing overheads, the margin of profit which can be earned on advances is of paramount importance. Interest on advances is the main source of bank revenue to meet outgoings and, although healthy competition between banks ensures that rates are kept to a minimum, it would obviously be foolish to contemplate any advance at a known over-all loss. Where the safety of any advance is unquestioned because the borrower and/or the security is undoubted, the rate of interest will often be somewhat lower than that charged for accepting a higher risk or perhaps for advancing for a less acceptable purpose.

Adopting these three bare heads as the basic principles, it will be appreciated that to test any proposal on such lines it is necessary to consider innumerable factors. An analysis of these details can now be attempted.

a. *The Borrower.*

To be safe the advance must clearly be granted to a borrower in whom the lender may have every confidence, and it is a *sine qua non* of good lending never to afford any facility to a borrower upon whom the bank cannot rely, however strong may be the security. It is common knowledge that a good banker should know his customer and be able to judge not only his integrity but his ability to use the bank money to advantage and repay it within an acceptable period. Who is the borrower and what does the banker know of his business experience and integrity? What are the nature and prospects of his business in relation to economic conditions and needs? In short, is the potential borrower credit worthy?

The integrity of the borrower must be undoubted, particularly where the security is inadequate to cover the maximum to be advanced. Without confidence in the customer it is dangerous to make any advance. So many opportunities arise in banker-customer relationships to enable the borrower to take unfair advantage of the bank and other trade creditors. For example, losses can easily be hidden in trading accounts by over-valuation of stock, whilst assets covered by a floating charge may legally be sold and the proceeds used to meet pressing creditors or directors' salaries regardless of the bank position. In particular, unsecured lending and advances made against the pledge of produce call for unquestionable confidence in the integrity and co-operative dealing of the borrower.

What is known of the experience of the borrower? If a private trader or partner in a firm, has he made a success of the business to date? How long has he been engaged in this particular trade and what profits has he earned? Does he spend all the profit he makes or does he live prudently, leaving adequate margin for possible losses? Does he normally enjoy good health and possess drive and energy with ample capacity for hard work? If the borrower is a limited company, then in a similar manner the banker will wish to know whether the directors are men of experience, drive and integrity, whilst the past results of the company will give some indication of its success and prospects. These qualities of experience and drive are essential in current competitive conditions where the weaker producer or seller must ultimately be driven out.

It would be unwise to-day to share with an inexperienced borrower the obvious risks entailed in tapping or exploring a new market or business. The past record of any borrower is an invaluable guide. Why lend to enable any customer to embark upon a fresh project quite remote from his previous business training or experience?

Examples from practice are legion. One is the middle-aged retailer who tires of suburban life and decides to buy a farm where, in his opinion, quicker profits can be earned in more amenable surroundings. The capital outlay is covered from the customer's own resources but would a banker be wise to lend such a customer the balance required for working capital? Is it reasonable to expect success from such an inexperienced farmer? Perhaps the risk can be accepted when adequate security is available and the customer heeds the practical warnings given to him by the lending banker. But in normal circumstances it would be an imprudent advance. How often have banks been asked to finance customers in their purchase of a hotel or boarding-house business? To run any hotel successfully to-day requires much experience and constant attention. It is certainly not a venture for the inexperienced, although optimistic borrowers anxious to make their fortune in such pursuits still abound. No rules can be laid down because the merits and disadvantages of every proposal depend on so many factors, but the experience and previous record of any potential borrower are points demanding full weight when the proposal is on the scales.

Alas, those with undoubted trade experience, technical knowledge, energy, initiative and drive can nevertheless fail through lack of financial acumen. Consideration must also be given to the ability of the borrower to control the finances of the business. In a limited company one or more directors will perhaps be responsible for budgetary control, but in the case of a sole trader or small partnership it is often prudent to recommend the services of a local accountant to act as financial controller and adviser. Successful trading can still be ruined by haphazard financial control and an advance jeopardised by lack of care in costing and the granting of credit to buyers. It is a all matter of judgment. The successful cloth manufacturer may be completely ignorant of farming, but his financial acumen and resources more than suffice to enable his banker to grant advances to finance stock purchases for the farm. On the other hand, the technical expert in crops and the rearing of stock may be a more unsuitable borrower because of his complete failure to understand the need for budgetary control and skilled costing. The same principles apply to all forms of business. The weary clerk may not succeed in his venture as a window-cleaner despite his anxiety for fresh air and self-employment. On the other hand, the experienced market operator may become over-confident and in a gambling mood accept fatal risks. Sufficient has been said to indicate how imperative it is for every bank manager to know his customers and from such close knowledge of their experience, capacity and temperament to be able to assess their credit worthiness. Banking in this respect is still, and always will be, a very personal business based on mutual confidence and knowledge.

b. *The Business of the Borrower.*
Some thought must next be given to the nature and prospects of the business of the borrower, with particular reference to economic conditions. The natural optimism of every potential borrower has to be discounted and the real prospects of the venture coldly assessed in the light of known conditions. Allied with this enquiry is the desirability of the advance, but this aspect can be conveniently left for examination under a later heading. Here the field is limited to the possibility of success or otherwise of the venture for which finance is required from the bank. With the experience or otherwise of the borrower, is the project likely to succeed? If it fails, the bank will have to fall back on its security to recover its advances and the lending will be fundamentally unsound. If it succeeds, sufficient will be available from profits, after taxation, gradually to liquidate the bank debt. Is the money, therefore, required to support or expand an established business dealing in an essential market with an assured demand, or is it needed for a more speculative project with undeveloped markets or subject to the dictates of fashion or even the weather? In the former event, the position is sound, other factors being satisfactory, but in the latter case the risk must be one which a banker may prudently accept. In general, the business prospects of the borrower in the light of known and prospective conditions have to be weighed in the balance and heavy risks in such respect can usually be accepted only with experienced borrowers whose capital resources are adequate to cover unexpected losses. At this stage it is merely a matter of forming an independent opinion of the future of the venture which requires financial assistance. If that future is doubtful or the project is too much of a gamble, the money cannot be lent unless the weakness is completely overridden by other factors. The test is whether the bank manager in the given circumstances would be prepared to lend

his own money (instead of the depositors') in support of the project. The possible market for the goods, the likely demand at a satisfactory price and the risks of intervention or competition from others, all have to be considered. The facts can be thrashed out with the customer, whose knowledge of the problems will soon be appreciated. If the prospects have been thoroughly explored before the request is made for any advance, much more confidence will be engendered than where the customer seeks support without thought of the marketing and development problems to be overcome. Would anyone contentedly lend to a factor to market ice cream to the Eskimos, or woollen vests to equatorial natives? Between these extremes there is much to be considered by the banker in any proposal for accommodation required by a customer. Again, there are no tram lines demanding a prescribed course. It is a question of considering the business and its prospects in conjunction with all other factors and recording, as it were, a vote for or against the proposal.

c. *Capital Resources of the Borrower.*
Some customers expect their banker to provide most of the capital required in a business. Possessed of drive, knowledge, and the original idea, but little cash, the customer approaches the bank, instead of friends or the market, for the capital needed to float and run the enterprise. It is definitely not the function of a modern bank to find the capital or invest in the customer's business, and usually by far the major interest or stake should be that of the proprietors and/or long-term lenders. An excessive stake in a business means that the bank is accepting an undue risk at rates too fine to repay such a high risk. The liquid position of any potential borrower demands close assessment and the greater the bank debt, actual or prospective, in relation to the capital resources of the business the weaker inherently must be the financial position of the borrower who employs a portion of the short-term funds to buy fixed assets. As a general guide, a banker will rarely wish to lend more than the amount of the proprietor's capital, but there are exceptions to this tendency. For example, factors or brokers dealing with marketable produce in good demand may borrow several times more than their own capital on occasion from banks against the security of the produce, with or without collateral support. For our purpose, such cases are preferably regarded as distinct exceptions to a general rule. On the other hand, lack of capital in the business may be overcome from the banking standpoint by the deposit of adequate personal security by the proprietors. Instead of investing directly in their business, they support the bank debt with their own private assets.

d. *Amount Required.*
The amount required has to be considered not only in relation to the

capital resources of the borrower but also in relation to the purpose for which the overdraft is wanted. The inevitable question of "how much?" also entails the prudent query "is it sufficient?". The principle is clear in that it would be folly to agree to advance a maximum which is quite inadequate to finance the given project. A simple example proves this point. Builder customer Z requires £30,000 to assist in the finance of his erection of a pair of houses to cost £50,000. Z has working capital of £10,000 available and is satisfied that trade credit, plus deposits from the prospective buyers, will suffice to enable him to complete the scheme. The bank realises the finance budget is tight. There is no margin for any rise in the price of labour or materials or to cover delays which may occur through bad weather. The bank it may be assumed definitely regards an advance of £30,000 here as an absolute maximum. To lend more would be to accept an undue risk. Nevertheless, the facility is made available to Z against the sole security of the two houses in course of erection. The worst happens. With delays in building and rising costs, Z finds that after using up the agreed advance of £30,000 and exhausting all trade credit, he cannot buy the labour and materials to roof the properties. The bank has already advanced what is regarded as a prudent maximum, but its security is incomplete and in normal times unsaleable. No alternative remains but to increase the advance by a further £10,000 to complete the houses which may, with difficulty, realise barely sufficient to cover the bank debt. In this manner the bank was forced into an unsatisfactory position through failure to explore the field fully at the outset to ensure that the amount required, plus other resources including trade credit, would suffice to complete the project after due margin for rises in price, etc. In short, a finance budget should be prepared by the customer and analysed and criticised by the bank before deciding that the maximum overdraft needed is sufficient for the purpose. The depth of such enquiry will naturally vary according to the known ability and capital resources of the borrower in relation to the work to be done. In some cases it may not matter much whether the agreed maximum has later to be extended, but in the vast majority of proposals it is a vital factor. Here, again, prudence demands that the undue optimism of the average borrower is discounted and care taken to consider in the finance budget the effect of taxation upon the estimated cash resources of the customer. If undue reliance is placed on deferred credit to make up any shortage, there is the danger that overtrading may develop.

To decide whether the amount required is sufficient it is necessary to explore fully the whole purpose of the advance, which at the same time raises the question of suitability of the project. Is it a desirable purpose from the standpoint of the bank and in the best interests of the economic health of the nation? The manner in which all these principles are inter-related will now be appreciated.

e. *The Purpose of the Advance.*

Why is the stated banking accommodation required by the customer? The answer to this pertinent question demands full consideration because the purpose must be one which commands the support of the bank. If it is outside banking policy there will be no need to proceed further.

Is the money needed for a desirable purpose from the banking stand-point? Here again it is unwise to be dogmatic. There can be no unalterable list of acceptable or sound objects for bank lending. Every proposal has to be considered on its own merits in the light of all the other factors and it may be, for example, that on occasions an advance has to be made for an unsuitable purpose to avoid disturbing a valuable connection or incurring the wrath of a wealthy if turbulent customer, whose security margin commands respect. Ignoring such exceptions, the banker will not wish to lend to finance speculation or betting. Obviously, a loan of £500 to back an alleged certain winner in the big race is not banking business. From this extreme example the extent of speculation may gradually improve to the case of the skilled market operator buying produce in expectation of a rise in its price. Whilst in days of old a banker may have supported the wealthy stock market operator with ample security, such advances although profitable were not eminently desirable. The expert, however, who uses bank advances to buy heavily the goods in which he normally deals in expectation of a rise in price, is fulfilling a market function and ironing out the price fluctuations. To support such a borrower too far might lead to unsatisfactory stockpiling, but much must naturally depend on the nature of the goods and the banker's knowledge of the market. There is a wide difference between financing purchases of turkeys to meet Christmas demand (with cold stores to hold excess supplies) and finding the money to enable a speculative trader to corner the supply of panama hats for that perfect summer which is impatiently awaited. In short, it depends upon the nature of the business and the sureness of the project. To assist any trader or producer of essential goods to carry reasonable stocks is clearly a laudable banking object. It is normally most satisfactory business in that the advance is speedily repaid as the goods are sold and the money is retaken to replace the stocks, whilst profits earned by the customer in the process gradually reduce the peak borrowing figure. In short, the banker furnishes the working capital to the reliable borrower who is dealing in goods which are in reasonable demand and not unduly subject to the dictates of fashion or the whims of the relatively few wealthy buyers. The general test, therefore, is whether the bank is called upon to finance a reasonable business project buying or preparing to meet a known demand, or a mere speculation akin to a betting transaction.

In current conditions, with high taxation, the banker is often asked to lend to enable the trading customer to pay taxation. This is a reasonable purpose if the cash from the taxable profits has been employed as working capital in the business and can be realised in reasonable time to repay the bank debt. But where the profits have been used to buy fixed assets the bank advance will not be so self-liquidating and care is necessary to ensure that a long-term facility is not thereby created. It is no part of sound banking to furnish fixed capital, either directly or in this indirect manner. Likewise caution is necessary where advances are needed to repair the ravages of trade losses. If confidence in the borrower remains unimpaired and there is a sound prospect of future profit, it is clearly advisable to assist an old friend through the lean years, but in the absence of improved results fresh capital is the only solution. A distinction has to be made between financing losses and tiding a good borrower over a bad year or an isolated experience.

In general, requirements for capital outlay are not desirable banking business because they tend to be long-term advances repayable only gradually from surplus profits after tax and the satisfaction of the demands of the proprietors. Unless a reasonably speedy means of repayment can be seen, the borrower may be advised to seek more permanent finance or fresh capital. Much again will depend upon the capital position and detailed nature of the need. If a producer whose capital resources are already fully employed wishes to borrow to build and equip a factory extension, he probably needs a mortgage on the entire factory unless fresh capital can be attracted. On the other hand, another customer with adequate working capital may extend his factory by using all the available current resources, relying upon bank borrowing to carry stocks and finance production until accumulated profits restore the cash position. In such event, the bank debt would fluctuate according to daily needs with ample turnover. Advances to buy houses, hotels, ships, or to finance other heavy capital outlays are not *prima facie* desirable banking business, but much will depend upon the proportion of capital supplied by the borrower, the prospects for speed of repayment, and all the other factors reviewed, or to be reviewed, elsewhere in this book. Perhaps the safest summary is to say that mortgage finance is not alone desirable banking business.

Apart from the provision of working capital to sound trading customers, the most desirable banking business is probably the short-term bridgeover type of facility where the advance will be repaid from an undoubted known source within a reasonable time. It may cover a variety of transactions. The private customer may borrow to buy his house pending the arrangement of a building society mortgage. The father may borrow to balance his family budget pending the maturity of his life policy. Executors borrow to pay death duties until estate assets can be realised to liquidate their debt. The farmer borrows until the harvest. Examples of this principle abound. The test of all such self-liquidating proposals is naturally the degree of reliance which may be placed upon the source of repayment.

Will the required minimum be forthcoming on the given date? The facts alone will tell.

In short, judged solely from the standpoint of desirability of purpose a satisfactory banking advance is one which supports a sound, legal and moral short-term trading requirement or meets a similar private or professional need. Some proposals, of course, must be declined because they are *ultra vires* the borrower or otherwise illegal, but they are outside of this volume.

It is moreover, appropriate to note that over the major part of the last quarter of a century the purpose of any bank advance has also been a matter for Government control, both actual and persuasive. "Qualitative guidance" is given by the Bank of England from time to time to banks and deposit-taking finance houses prescribing the direction for bank lending towards the promotion of exports and the limitation of imports. Personal borrowing and advances for financial speculation are given low priority.

Since 1971 the Authorities have relied upon overall control of total bank lending, within a general policy of constraint on monetary aggregates, using an ability to call for special deposits (compulsory deposits on interest-bearing accounts at the central bank) and the supplementary special deposit scheme (penal amounts required for deposit at the Bank of England should the lender's interest-bearing liabilities exceed a minimum amount). This latter arrangement has been introduced to control un-fettered access to the money markets by the banks where funds can be borrowed for further advances to customers thus generating new money flows and stoking inflation.

f. *The Source of Repayment.*

The next question concerns the liquidity of the advance. Being satisfied that a sufficient amount required to meet the precise needs of a satisfactory borrower with adequate capital resources relative to the project is to be taken for an approved purpose, the prudent banker will wish to know how long the advance is likely to outstand and from what source it is to be reduced and eventually repaid. The need for liquidity and the essential short-term nature of bank advances has already been emphasised. To complete the picture, the means of repayment demand consideration and a distinction can perhaps be made between the following three general types of advances.

1. The pure bridge-over facility pending a known receipt.
2. The provision of additional working capital for normal trade requirements.
3. The longer term advance subject to reduction over a period.

A bridge-over facility presents little difficulty because the source and likely date of repayment can be determined with reasonable accuracy at the outset. Undoubted borrowers may indulge in capital outlay with bank support pending a capital or debenture issue, or the arrangement of mortgage finance, and their plans will be made ahead. The private customer may borrow pending maturity of a life policy, receipt of a legacy from a deceased's estate, the redemption or sale of given shares. In every case the banker can verify the facts and judge the reliability of the means of repayment. They are reasonably certain and the term of such an advance must vary according to the view taken by the bank of all the other interdependent principles which have already been discussed.

Advances made to a sound borrower to support normal trading requirements will be repaid in the ordinary course of business as the trade cycle of the borrower revolves. For example, where the retailer or wholesaler borrows to increase his stocks, the bank will be repaid from the proceeds of sale of the goods. The ability of such a borrower to buy the right goods and to dispose of them within a reasonable time in the right market has been discussed. If the banker has no confidence in the borrower in this respect, the prospect of speedy repayment will obviously be thought remote. In other words, the source of repayment of this type of an advance hinges on the other principles of lending. If they are satisfactory, the advance will be self-liquidating and the speed of turnover will vary according to the nature of the business upon which the borrower is engaged. If there is any weakness, however, stockpiling, or overtrading with forced realisations will ensue. The sound borrower within this category will often have an overdraft limit placed at his disposal for use as required. By the operation of the Rule in *Clayton's Case* it will be repaid every month or every quarter, as the case may be, and providing the turnover is well maintained and the profit record and capital position, etc., of the borrower continues beyond reproach, the banker is unlikely to call for any reduction in the agreed maximum. In effect a more or less permanent arrangement is evolved always subject, of course, to periodic review. In theory, the degree of support required from the bank should decrease as profits are accumulated.

One word of warning with regard to trade advances to customers engaged in contract work subject to retentions. A builder or other contractor may undertake large scale contracts obtaining periodic progress payments for work done, but the employer may withhold a proportion of the amount so due until the work has been completed to his satisfaction. The full value of labour and materials spent by such a borrower is not, therefore, automatically recovered. A proportion of his outlay, including profit, is frozen for the time being in retentions. The amount involved may be as much as 20 per cent. of the contract figure and it may be retained in whole or in part for as long as one year after the termination of the work. This aspect obviously demands close consideration. Has the borrower adequate capital resources to afford the retentions, relying only on bank advances for the outlay which can be repaid from regular progress payments? Here, again, the dangers of overtrading are ever present. The tests are simple. How much has to be paid out in labour and materials and how much can be recovered at the end of a given period by way of progress payments? As the contract proceeds the amount frozen in retentions will increase. Are the resources of the borrower sufficient to finance the retentions? Many contractors engaged on such work to-day have considerable revolving sums tied up in retentions.

Lastly, it is well to consider that class of advance which is subject to repayment over a period. Although primarily a short-term lender demanding liquidity of advances, the banker on occasion may support a suitable customer in a capital or semi-capital project, or may grant exceptional facilities to a customer whose working capital is sadly depleted. Advances within this category must be subject to a scheme for periodic reduction to permit of repayment within a reasonable period. The proposed length of the advance and the speed of reduction must depend upon the facts of each case. It may be that a private customer with adequate resources can be assisted exceptionally in some capital outlay, but the amount advanced will be limited to a figure which the borrower should be able to wipe-off over a few years. Cover against death in the interim will usually be required and the prospect of repayment rests on the margin calculated between known net income and likely living costs. It is hardly necessary to point out that nowadays with heavy taxation this margin is usually very small and the prospect of repayment from such a source is correspondingly doubtful.

Perhaps a manufacturer, trader, farmer or hotel proprietor may merit support to buy machinery, a shop, a farm, or a hotel but all such advances will be on a reducing basis. Moreover, the speed of reduction, usually in annual instalments, will generally be much more rapid than that required by a building society or kindred lender. It is in these cases where the optimism of the customer knows no bounds. The only source of reduction is from profits earned and they are still subject to heavy taxation. The net surplus remaining after satisfying the demands of the Inland Revenue and allowing a suitable reward to the borrower is rarely sufficient to permit of speedy reduction. Care is necessary to impress upon the optimistic borrower the incidence of taxation. The earning capacity of the business can often be judged from past results in relation to business prospects in the particular trade and the known ability of the borrower, but the fact that the profit has first to be made and tax paid thereon before anything remains to reduce the bank debt must never be forgotten. The security may well be adequate, but the prudent banker wishes to see a reasonable source of repayment without recourse to the security. Borrowers of this type must show a real prospect of repayment from profits and budget for regular reduction to be achieved from net profits before thought of other outlay. The best and apparently safest schemes can be completely upset or seriously retarded by bad trading years arising from circumstances outside the control of the borrower. Earning capacity and trading prospects have then to be weighed seriously in the balance and the reduction schedule based on the most pessimistic estimate. If reductions calculated on this basis are inadequate for the bank purpose, it is usually wiser to decline to advance rather than to dream of reductions beyond the reach of the customer.

Incidentally, in many weaker cases where for special reasons the bank decides to accept an undue risk, it is helpful to both the customer and the bank if the accommodation is taken on loan account subject to monthly or quarterly reduction by standing arrangement from a current account maintained by the borrower strictly on a creditor basis. In this manner the customer knows the extent of his cash resources and realises that in the current account he has to build up a reserve to meet the transfer to the loan account due on the agreed date. Properly managed, the loan is gradually funded in this manner without irregularities which may otherwise be caused when pressing for reduction of an overdrawn current account. The control is closer and the psychological effect on the borrower is more salutary.

The moral throughout is not to advance unless there is a reliable source of repayment within a reasonable time and, in considering such prospect, due margin must be allowed in the budget for imponderables. Above all, the natural optimism of the average customer has to be discounted and the incidence of tax ever kept in the limelight. The surplus for reduction must come from net profits, leaving sufficient remaining to continue the business successfully on the same, if not increased, scale of operations. To rely upon reductions from the forced sale of stocks or by closing down parts of the business is normally to invite the failure of the borrower. Better not to lend at all.

g. *Security.*
Almost the last point for consideration is that of security. Many customers in ignorance perhaps of the true functions of a bank think that loans are made against security. This is clearly incorrect. If the principles of lending which have been discussed justify the assistance of a customer, then the security will be obtained as a form of insurance against any unforseen development. The best plans can go astray and, as the accommodation is financed from deposits, security is taken as a final safeguard. If the proposal does not commend itself to the banker on other grounds no amount of security alone will enable the customer to borrow from the bank, but a much greater risk can obviously be accepted if there is ample security available to cover the advance.

It follows that the prudent bank lender will always endeavour to obtain the maximum security available from the borrower. There must usually be sufficient margin to provide against fluctuations in value, but it is a good principle to prevail upon the customer to charge at the outset everything available and acceptable to the bank, thereby obtaining sufficient in case of need to extend the facilities without squeezing fresh security, and also limiting the possibility that the customer, unknown to the bank, may later borrow against security from other sources and so indirectly endanger the bank's position. Such policy of perfection cannot always be implemented but it is essential to avoid the impression that the loan is merely against the given security. Actually the advance is granted because the bank has confidence in the ability of the borrower to use the money to advantage for the given approved purpose and to repay it from an acknowledged source within a reasonable term. Any enquiry from the customer as to how much the bank will lend against the stated security should immediately be corrected. The question is how much is required to achieve the customer's purpose and what security is available for such otherwise satisfactory borrowing.

The advantages and disadvantages of the various types of banking security and the distinction between direct and collateral cover are beyond the scope of this short book, but it is prudent here to emphasise that the best security is of little value if it cannot be realised without difficulty when an emergency arises. The title obtained by the bank to any security must, therefore, be perfect and the value of the security maintained as far as possible throughout the advance. Few securities can be taken and virtually forgotten. A constant watch of the value of quoted shares is clearly desirable. In the case of property, care is necessary to ensure that it is properly maintained and always fully insured against all known risks. With life policies, premiums have to be paid promptly, and with guarantees the standing of the guarantor has to be verified regularly. Constant care and attention must, therefore, be devoted throughout the history of the advance to the state and value of the security. It is a vital part of the entire lending operation. Accepting these principles, the details can be left for study in the separate book in this series which is devoted to the subject.

Borrowers sometimes object to meeting incidental costs entailed in the creation of a legal mortgage as security and expect the bank instead to be content with an informal deposit or equitable mortgage. Such attempts to weaken the bank position cannot be justified solely on the grounds of saving costs and have to be resisted. Other lenders will certainly demand completed security or decline to make the advance, and compared with the rewards the customer will earn from the use of the accommodation these costs are negligible. It is all a matter for negotiation according to the circumstances, but the golden rule is that the security should be completely charged to the bank to endow it with every legal right for use without recourse to the borrower whenever the need arises.

c

h. *Profitability.*

Lastly, regard must be paid to the profit to be derived from the advance, which must therefore be granted at a satisfactory rate of interest in relation to the risk entailed. Borrowing from a bank on overdraft with interest calculated on the daily cleared balance is usually much cheaper than a long term loan of fixed amount taken at a lower rate than that charged by the bank. If a customer borrows say £5,000 on outside mortgage at 8½ per cent., it will cost £425 gross per year and he may at times carry a credit balance of £500/600 at his bank. An overdraft facility enabling him to borrow as and when required up to a maximum of £5,000 with interest at say 2 per cent. over the bank's Base rate, may cost much less over the year because the actual daily indebtedness is smaller than £5,000 on average. This aspect of bank borrowing is not always appreciated by customers.

The rate quoted by the bank will naturally vary according to the strength of the customer, the nature and value of the security and the size of the facility. There may be other considerations but, in general, the greater the risk the higher the rate, always remembering that it is not the function of a bank to accept an undue risk merely for a high reward. Lending rates are competitive and the dissatisfied customer can always seek cheaper accommodation elsewhere. If the money is urgently required by the customer in his business, he must expect to pay the appropriate market rate, which it must be emphasised is merely the price paid for the use of the money and in no manner contributes to the cost of providing the other banking services enjoyed by the borrower. Such services are paid for by way of commission or service charge, which is quite distinct from the debit interest.

The rate quoted will usually vary according to the Base rate of the lending bank. It would be unwise to quote a fixed rate which may quickly become unremunerative by reason of changes in money market conditions. A careless statement that the bank will lend at say 6 per cent. will soon occasion trouble if, for example, Base rate is increased to 7 per cent. in the following year. A bank always lends at a certain rate per cent. over its Base rate. Where any advance is granted at a fixed rate an increase has to be negotiated with the borrower and, although as a last resort an unremunerative advance could be called in on demand, it is hardly the best method of maintaining a happy business relationship with the customer. Far better to quote the rate properly at the outset.

FINAL SUMMARY

This completes the review of the basic principles of bank lending and, to summarise all the features which have been discussed, it will be realised that the information to be collated by the branch manager at his initial interview with the potential borrower includes the following:

1. Who is the borrower and what is known of his ability, integrity and experience in the particular business? What are the general prospects in his trade or profession? Do the borrower and his business inspire confidence? Much of this information will be known to the branch manager before the interview.
2. How much is required? Is it sufficient, coupled with other resources available to the borrower, to enable him to achieve the given purpose? Has adequate margin been allowed for possible increases in cost? Is the relationship between the maximum advance and the existing capital resources of the borrower reasonable or is the customer expecting the bank to provide too large a stake in his business? Will the liquid position of the borrower remain satisfactory after the full advance has been taken?
3. What is the purpose of the advance? Is it a project which commends itself to banking functions or is it a long term capital outlay more suited to a specialist lender?
4. How long will it be before the advance can be repaid? Is it a reasonable short term borrowing? What is the source of repayment and when is it likely to be made? Is the proposal sufficiently liquid?
5. What security is available? Is it satisfactory? Is the value sufficient to furnish the desired margin? Can a valid title be obtained? Are there any weaknesses? Can the security be perfected before the advance is taken?
6. To agree the appropriate rate for the facility and to discuss any other business arising out of the proposal.

After collation of these facts, often with an exhaustive analysis of the balance sheet of the borrower, the branch manager will be able to appreciate the risk and decide whether or not the advance can be granted. Without such appreciation the lending would be made blind and the result left to chance, constituting bad banking. It by no means follows that every point must be satisfactory to commend the proposal. Expediency may well demand that to foster a connection or to support a deserving case risks have to be accepted under various headings. The security may be quite inadequate but the confidence in the borrower and his trade prospects may outweigh such defects. The advance may be for a longer term than normal, but the customer's standing and connection may warrant the acceptance of the business. It depends entirely on the facts with due regard to the competitive factor which fortunately still prevails for the benefit of the customer. The essentials have been outlined for general guidance and the degree to which they are followed must vary according to the proposal under consideration. The art of banking is surely to know when to accept the risk. But the able banker at the outset must be able to appreciate and assess that risk.

Chapter III

Unsecured Advances

NO BALANCE SHEET AVAILABLE

Having outlined the general principles of lending, an attempt will now be made to apply them to typical practical problems and it is convenient to start the survey with a discussion of the risks of unsecured advances. How can they be measured? Why and when should they be accepted? A distinction must first be drawn between the unsecured advance to a private or a professional customer and unsecured facilities made available to trading customers for their business requirements. There is a vast difference between these two types of lending from the standpoint both of evidence available to support the proposal and of risk.

THE PRIVATE BORROWER

As a general rule it is bad banking to grant unsecured advances to a private borrower unless there can be no doubt concerning his capital resources in relation to the amount borrowed and his outside liabilities. In theory, the counsel of perfection is never to lend without adequate security to a private customer, but in practice competition often demands the acceptance of a real risk perhaps to preserve a connection or to help a deserving customer over a lean time. No unbreakable rules can be laid down because each case must be judged according to its merits. Some basic principles can, however, be discussed to advantage for general guidance.

When considering an approach from a private customer for unsecured accommodation, the following essential features usually have to be weighed in the balance.

1. The income of the potential borrower, whether earned and/or unearned, will cease at death, which regardless of his apparent good health may happen unexpectedly through an accident.

2. What are his known free resources? If ample, why is it that security cannot be furnished?

3. There may be substantial private creditors who would rank *pari passu* with the bank in the event of failure. The preferential claims of the Inland Revenue for unpaid income tax and surtax may often be heavy.

4. Does the connection or standing of the customer nevertheless warrant acceptance of these risks? Is the business of the bank likely

to benefit directly or indirectly by assisting the customer regardless of the prudent canons of bank lending?

These aspects will be discussed in greater detail in Chapter XII when formalised personal lending is referred to. We can, however, quite separately from this type of loan, now examine some typical examples of unsecured overdrafts.

Firstly, there is the wealthy customer whose financial standing is beyond doubt. He lives well on earned and unearned income and has a widespread business connection, being on the boards of several well known companies. The deeds of his estate and his stocks and shares are all held in safe custody. Nevertheless, in these days of high living costs and heavy taxation there is unlikely to be much margin between his income and expenditure. When he has occasion to borrow from the bank, he declines to furnish security. Any suggestion of security is abhorrent to him and he confidently expects the bank to follow his requirements without even enquiring too deeply into the reason for the borrowing, and the source of repayment. Obviously such customers have to be handled with the greatest care. To upset them may endanger a profitable company connection. This is where the real test of good banking arises. The branch manager has to decide on the one hand just how far he may meet the wishes of the customer unsecured, and on the other hand how he can obtain security without causing umbrage. To know how far to press in the course of negotiations demands a nicety of judgment and great tact. It depends entirely upon personal knowledge of the customer and affords an excellent example of how essential it is for every branch manager to know his customers. One false step may cause umbrage and damage the connection. Failure to attempt to negotiate may entail ultimate loss to the bank. In general, however, little risk arises where ample free assets are held by the bank and the borrowing is temporary pending receipt of known income (a dividend on a major holding due in a few weeks) or the maturity of a life policy or the redemption of certain stock. Ideally, all advances without security to this type of customer should be short term bridge-over facilities. It is not the function of the banker to carry an increasing debt arising from regular spending in excess of income. From the standpoint of both banking policy and sound private finance, capital should be realised to cover the excess outlay and thereafter economy introduced to balance the private budget. To finance large scale private capital outlay—a new house—a new investment—by borrowing long term from the bank is clearly contrary to the basic principles but where it is possible to entertain such a requirement it should be on a fully secured basis.

Whilst the temporary needs of a customer with known capital resources, good standing and connection merit favourable consideration without security, the demands of the spendthrift or remittance man who habitually expects the bank to tide him over an alleged temporary stringency can obviously be dismissed without much thought. It is no part of the function of a banker to accept such risks and, if the customer is foolish enough to anticipate his income he must seek assistance from those specialist lenders who charge appropriately for the willing acceptance of a high risk.

Then there is the employee customer with limited capital resources who occasionally approaches the bank for assistance. After due allowance for the incidence of taxation, there can be little margin between his net income and expenditure, but he hopes the bank will treat him sympathetically and either tide him over a financial stress arising from circumstances outside his control or perhaps enable him to seize an opportunity to acquire a special investment in the company by whom he is employed. The income of such a customer ceases at death and, unless adequate life cover has been taken out and is maintained out of income, there is no means available to the bank of recovering the debt outstanding at death. Moreover, the proceeds of such life policies may all be needed to repay the bank, leaving the dependants virtually penniless. Is the customer wise even to contemplate the borrowing? It may be, however, that through family sickness, the cost of an operation or special medical treatment for his wife or children, he has little alternative but to seek help from the bank. Whilst it may not be banking business and the degree to which the banker can allow sympathy to weigh his decision is very limited, some cases may merit exceptional consideration. Again, it depends entirely on the branch manager's knowledge of the customer. Is he of undoubted integrity and can he be relied upon to economise, and to maintain a reasonable scheme of monthly reduction? How long has he been a customer? Perhaps his family have banked with the branch over the past century. Does past experience with the customer demand sympathetic treatment in his hour of dire need? It may be that after weighing all the factors in the balance the banker will decide to accept the risk, assuming always that the amount required is reasonably small. But usually in such circumstances some form of life cover will be expected from the borrower. Unsecured advances granted largely on sympathetic grounds are exceptional. When granted, the banker should analyse the income and personal commitments of the borrower from a complete family budget furnished by the customer and endeavour to draw-up a scheme for funding the debt by monthly instalments. It is senseless to attempt a scheme which is beyond the income of the borrower and if prepared to accept the risk, the bank must usually accept an extended scheme for repayment. This type of facility is best taken on loan account reduced by an agreed amount each month by transfer from the current account of the borrower, usually on salary day.

THE PROFESSIONAL CUSTOMER
Sometimes the professional type of customer with inadequate capital

resources may seek unsecured accommodation. A young solicitor may wish to borrow to acquire a share in an established practice. He has little or no security to offer and cannot find any collateral support from relatives or friends. Strictly speaking, such capital outlay should be found entirely by the customer himself, but the firm concerned may be good friends of the bank and when their new partner settles down he may be in a position to introduce further business to the bank. His requirements, therefore, demand every consideration. The bank money in effect will be invested in the firm of solicitors and, assuming it prospers, will be recoverable in the event of the death of the new partner. On the other hand, prudence demands that the young man should take out a life policy for the maximum amount required from the bank, assuming always that he can finance the premiums comfortably from expected income. If a satisfactory scheme of repayment can also be arranged, the risk may well be acceptable. Much will depend upon what proportion of the purchase price the customer can find from his own resources (he can hardly expect the bank to find the whole amount) the prospects of the firm (which may be long established), and the speed of repayment. With a life policy in the background to cover in the event of death, it may be expedient to grant the unsecured advance.

In like manner, an accountant may require assistance to furnish an office extension or to carry the practice over the year end pending receipt of fees from clients. No security is available. The assets of the business largely comprise debtors for fees with few trade creditors. Fixed assets usually will be negligible and of doubtful forced sale value. The goodwill of the connection, although intangible, is the only likely other source of repayment in the event of the unexpected death of the borrower. But such a professional customer may have a sound connection of indirect value to the bank and expediency may demand that temporary unsecured assistance be granted to make-up his deficiency in capital. Again, much must hinge upon the banker's knowledge of the customer, his local standing, method of living, ability and prospects. It would obviously be unwise to support a practice decaying through the neglect or weakness of the proprietor, and it would be equally foolish to decline to help a progressive young man building up an expanding connection. Generally, if the basic principles of lending fit the proposal such a customer warrants assistance without security, but a life policy in the background to insure against the death of the borrower is helpful.

The reputation and skill of other young professional customers, such as journalists, surgeons, barristers and actors, are often the only assets they possess. As such personal assets are inherent in the customer and die with him, limited unsecured assistance can usually be granted only when the banker has unbounded confidence in the future earning capacity of the borrower, to enable him to repay, and a life policy is charged in support.

Even then these advances are rarely sound banking proposals and probably excused on the grounds of expediency.

UNSATISFACTORY CUSTOMERS

Lastly, a word of warning concerning the unsatisfactory private customer who persists in anticipating dividend or salary receipts and thereby obtains unsecured facilities without the express approval of the bank. Unless the customer has known free resources of sufficient value to justify such irregularities, it is dangerous to allow any private customer to help himself to the bank moneys. Each case must be dealt with according to the circumstances, but no customer is entitled to overdraw his account without prior arrangement with his banker. The salaried official with slender resources who is short at the end of each month may soon rely upon the bank regularly to make-up the deficiency if no objection has been raised to his excess drawings in previous months. The initial small excesses become a monthly habit and tend gradually to increase in amount, whilst an implied arrangement is thereby established between the customer and the banker. Unless disciplinary action is taken at the outset and the customer warned that he may not overdraw, it may later be difficult to dishonour cheques in order to correct the position. The customer might rightly contend that as the bank had allowed him to overdraw up to say £30 for a few days each month from March to July they could not in August refuse to pay a cheque which would make the account overdrawn £28. Thus, in effect, the customer may obtain small unsecured facilities which the bank would not otherwise have been disposed to allow, and with the obvious narrow margin, if any, between the income and expenditure of such a customer it may be several years before he can manage without help from the bank. Often debts created in his happy-go-lucky manner become irrecoverable and, although small for one account, the total loss throughout one bank might be appreciable, if, for example, one such bad debt was incurred each half-year at every branch in the system. Similar losses can arise through carelessness in allowing improvident customers to draw against uncleared effects. The net result is in fact an unsecured advance granted without consideration and prior approval.

CROSS-FIRING OPERATIONS

To complete the warning against the weak customer who obtains unsecured accommodation by devious means, reference must be made to the dangers of cross-firing operations. They can be carried out so easily where insufficient care is exercised in watching the transactions on the account.

Take a simple example where a customer conducts such operations personally through two accounts in his own name at different banks or branches. Suppose X has an account at Northtown Bank and another account at Southtown Bank. He is in dire need of money to meet pressing creditors but the balance of his accounts at both banks is exhausted. If he draws a cheque for £50 on Northtown Bank and pays it in to the credit of his account at Southtown, the balance at the latter bank will be credit £50 uncleared, but in the normal course the cheque on Northtown Bank will not be presented for payment for three days (or even four days if a weekend intervenes). Assuming next that Southtown Bank officials fail to note the drawer of the cheque or are otherwise unperturbed and allow X to draw against uncleared effects, the cheque which he has previously issued to Z for £48 may well be paid upon presentation on the same day. X by this ruse has placed his account in funds. He now has to provide for the cheque drawn on Northtown Bank and, failing to collect surplus moneys from other sources, he merely reverses the process and credits his account at Northtown with a cheque for £50 down on Southtown Bank. If he is again fortunate enough to escape notice, the original cheque will be paid against the uncleared credit and he is left to redress the position three days later at Southtown Bank. Expressed in this simple manner the scheme is obvious and readers may, with reason, enquire how the officials of either bank could be foolish enough to let such patent kite-flying transactions pass through their books. But where the cross-firing operations are merged with other transactions on an active account, they may escape detection for some time. The cure lies in a close examination of the paid cheques of the branch each day, treating with suspicion any cheque drawn by the customer payable to himself bearing the crossing of another bank or branch. If the relative account then discloses that the customer has been drawing against uncleared effects, the danger signals are bright and, apart from insisting that in future that customer may draw only against cleared effects, instructions should be given for the special direct presentation with wire or telephonic fate of any cheques received for collection which are drawn by the customer on other banks or branches. Immediate action of this kind will explode the scheme before it has reached sizeable proportions and, although one bank may perhaps then sustain a small loss (having paid against one of the uncleared cross entries) it is usually a happy relief from what may otherwise have serious consequences.

The basic principles are clear, but where the system is extended by the use of fictitious names and accounts and the fraud is carried out by a trader known to be engaged in an apparently healthy business and capable of winning the confidence of the bank managers concerned, the operations may for a time escape detection. For example, if our friend X was conducting an active wholesale business and aided by a plausible tongue gained the confidence of the manager, he could bolster his trading account by crediting thereto items drawn by himself or by friends or associates on accounts opened at various other banks in fictitious names. If he was allowed to draw against uncleared effects, the uncleared balance on the trading account might at any given time include several cheques for appreciable figures which were completely uncovered in the fictitious accounts on which they were drawn at other banks. To enable these cheques to be paid upon presentation, X has to draw on his trading account in favour of each fictitious or confederate name and apply those cheques to the accounts in time to meet the cheques coming forward for collection from his main banker. Thus he has to be able to draw against uncleared effects at all banks. Whether and for how long he can succeed in such operations also depends upon how quickly the banks concerned link the operations together. Obviously where a cheque drawn by say M in favour of P is covered by a cheque drawn by P in favour of M there are grounds for suspicion. The system is, however, less easy to detect where there is a circulatory movement allegedly backed by trading transactions. If X puts his account in funds by drawing on the account of P and then fixes P's account by drawing on M at yet another bank, he can perhaps correct M's account by a cheque drawn on the first account. But the recurrence of such entries should arouse the suspicion of the banker of M. The possible ramifications are nevertheless enough to warn any bank of the dangers of allowing a customer to draw regularly against uncleared effects and so to enjoy unsecured accommodation without express approval. The occasional exception granted where the drawers of the cheques paid in are well known names of undoubted standing is, of course, a different matter.

Where there is the slightest suggestion of any cross-firing operations, the manager of the bank whose suspicions are first aroused should communicate in confidence with the manager of the other bank, or branch, and they can then arrange together to watch their respective accounts in order to stop the scheme before it can develop.

To quote Lord Goddard, C. J., in *Rex* v. *Kritz* ([1949] 2 All E.R. 406) :— "Drawing against uncleared cheques is one of the oldest forms of fraud. Generally bank managers are too much on their guard to let it go on, but in this case, because of the specious lies which the appellant told the bank manager . . . the appellant managed to defraud the bank to a very considerable extent." In this case the customer cloaked his transactions by representing that he was engaged upon large deals in whisky and persuaded a number of people of straw to write cheques for sums which they never expected to possess. These worthless documents were then paid into the bank so that they could be drawn against before clearance. A means of obtaining unsecured accommodation which is fraught with danger to the bank.

This concludes a brief review of unsecured lending granted without the perusal of the borrower's balance sheet, which is the evidence normally available to a banker to whom approach is made for accommodation by a trading customer.

Chapter IV

Balance Sheets and the Banker

INTRODUCTORY FEATURES

It is time now to consider the guidance and information that a banker can obtain from an analysis of a customer's balance sheet. No one can deny the importance of readily understanding the summarised statement of affairs of any customer, whether that of a sole trader, a firm, or a limited company. Whilst essential to enable the banker to appreciate the possible risk when lending wholly or partly unsecured, this can also be helpful when lending against full security or merely to follow the fortunes of a creditor customer. The need always to know your customer has already been emphasised. Apart from the personal qualities of integrity, drive and experience, inherent in the individual director, partner, or sole trader, the value of knowing the financial strength of the customer as evidenced in the balance sheet is equally important and nowadays most customers greatly appreciate the action of their bankers in displaying an intelligent interest in their progress and financial problems. In short, the prudent branch manager will not only get to know his customer but he will also acquire a working knowledge of the customer's balance sheet, which can always be surveyed to advantage on the lines described below.

Although it may be necessary from time to time to mention accounting practice these pages will largely be confined to an explanation of the invaluable information and assistance the practical banker can derive from a balance sheet, which undoubtedly is a veritable fount of knowledge to form a sound basis for dealing with a customer. The stability of the business can be seen at a glance and, provided the balance sheet is fully understood, valuable data can be extracted and tactful questions asked which will lay bare the facts behind the figures.

Unfortunately, to many people a balance sheet remains an impenetrable mystery largely because they do not trouble to analyse the contents and study the construction thereof, and yet all that is required is an elementary knowledge of book-keeping and an understanding of company law when dealing with the balance sheet of a limited company.

BALANCE SHEET DEFINED

Accepting the risk of undue simplicity, an attempt must first be made to define a balance sheet. The usual definition, viz., "a statement of liabilities and assets" is, strictly speaking, incomplete, because items are often included on each side of the statement which cannot be regarded as assets or liabilities. A more complete definition is that a balance sheet is a classified summary of the ledger balances outstanding in a set of books after all the receipts and expenses applicable to the period to date have been transferred to trading or profit and loss account. These remaining balances are listed on a sheet of paper and arranged so as to show the liabilities on one side and the assets on the other. In any typical business at the end of a trading period, or whenever else the proprietors may wish, the expenses—rent, rates, wages, and salaries, purchases, and other costs—are debited to trading and profit and loss account, whilst all receipts from sales, investment income, discounts, etc., are credited to that account. Such transfers close off the revenue accounts, leaving debit balances in other accounts representing assets, and credit balances being liabilities. These outstanding balances can then be condensed and classified to constitute the balance sheet. It is not a ledger account and balances cannot therefore be transferred to it.

OBTAINING THE BALANCE SHEET

The first essential is, of course, to obtain the customer's balance sheet for perusal and return, a copy being made (if prints are not available) whilst it is in the banker's possession. If the banker enjoys, as he should, the confidence of the customer, the figures will be produced without question immediately they are available. But should a private trader or a partner object to producing the statement, there is no remedy other than to decline to grant or continue the advance without such evidence of the financial position. In the case of any limited company, other than an exempt private company, a search can always be made, if need be, at Companies House and the necessary information obtained therefrom. A limited company is bound by the Companies Act, 1948, to file a copy of its balance sheet with every annual return, and this can be examined personally in the files by a representative of the bank upon payment of a fee of five new pence. Such course will rarely be necessary as few directors will decline to furnish their bankers with evidence of the strength of their company.

DATE OF BALANCE SHEET

There is obviously little point in studying ancient history as a reliable guide to the current position and the balance sheet under review must therefore always be as up-to-date as possible. In the normal way it is an annual event compiled at the end of the trading year, but the figures may be extracted half-yearly, or weekly, or whenever the proprietors of the business may decide.

The private trader and partnership have to close their accounts annually to ascertain their profit or loss for tax purposes. The partnership will follow the rules in its articles, if any, or the time will be chosen by mutual consent of the partners. After all, there is always the Inland Revenue, the uninvited and sleeping partner of all concerns, in the background awaiting its share of the profits for the fiscal year. A limited company will make up its accounts for the peroid specified in its Articles of Association, and by virtue of the Companies Act, 1948, the directors of every company must at some date not later than eighteen months after the incorporation of the company and subsequently at least once in every calendar year draw up a profit and loss account, or an income and expenditure account in the case of a company not trading. This must be laid before the company in general meeting, together with a balance sheet as at the date to which the profit and loss account is made up. Hence a balance sheet is usually an annual event, although some organisations draw up one at the end of each half of their trading year.

The first essential upon receipt of a balance sheet is to note the date upon which the figures were extracted from the books of the customer. A balance sheet is never headed "for the year ended . . ." because it shows the position at a given time. The correct description is therfore "balance sheet as at . . .". As the auditor requires time in which to complete his examination of the books it is rarely possible to obtain a balance sheet within six weeks of the end of the trading period. Moreover, delays in publication may occur whilst tax provisions are considered by the auditors. In normal conditions the time lag between the date of the balance sheet and the completion of the audit will vary but little, and it is useful to maintain a diary showing the date of the balance sheet and the date of the auditor's certificate in each case. This will serve as a guide indicating when the next balance sheet is likely to be available and will avoid premature requests which are apt to annoy the customer or his accountant. It also follows that overdraft arrangements should, as far as possible be reviewed shortly after the production of the balance sheet so that prompt action may be taken where the figures disclose any material weakness or a general deterioration in the borrower's position.

At the time of writing a national debate is continuing on the use of inflation accounting as a means of adjusting balance sheet figures to allow fully for the ravages of inflation. The subject is a wide and complex one which is largely outside the range of this book. The reader may, however, soon see dual accounts being published by well-known companies in the United Kingdom. Comparison of the two sets of accounts, are constructed on the time-honoured historical accounting basis and the other allowing for inflation, will show some of the implications of this new form of balance sheet.

AUDITOR'S CERTIFICATE

The next point is to examine the auditor's certificate. If the balance sheet has not been compiled by a qualified accountant, the lender cannot have complete confidence in the figures. This is no reflection upon the integrity of the borrower, who may well have drawn up his balance sheet in complete good faith. But ignorance of book-keeping and accounting principles may result in an incorrect summary of the position. A statement drawn up by the customer without professional assistance is best looked upon as a general guide and acceptable as a basis for unsecured advances only where the figures have been carefully analysed in discussion with the customer. The successful retailer or farmer will probably be the first to admit that he is not an expert accountant, and such understandable faults as the inclusion in the stock figure of goods recently delivered but the omission of their cost from the total of creditors (because no account has yet been rendered) can occur to distort the true position. Each case must be judged upon its merits and as counsellor and friend the banker will nowadays advise his customer to enlist the services of an accountant who, quite apart from the audit, can do much perhaps to help from the taxation standpoint.

The balance sheet of every limited company must be audited and bear the auditor's report stating whether or not he has obtained all the information and explanations he has required and whether, in his opinion, the balance sheet is properly drawn up so as to exhibit the true and fair view of the company's affairs. No official or director of a limited company is allowed to act as its auditor and with the exception of an exempt private company a partner or employee of an officer of a company is likewise barred from such a position.

The auditor's certificate should always be studied with care in case any important qualifications are contained therein. It is unwise to accept the certificate as read even though in the vast majority of cases a clean certificate is given. For example, the depreciation on certain fixed assets may be considered inadequate or the accountant may advise further provision for bad and doubtful debts, and these factors have to be borne in mind when the relative figures are analysed.

Sometimes the banker may be asked to consider a proposal on the basis of draft or interim figures which reveal a much more up-to-date position, but are not audited. The degree of reliance which can be placed on such figures necessarily varies according to circumstances, but where deemed prudent the borrower's accountant can always be asked to verify them to a certain limited extent. At times the banker may seek the customer's permission to discuss the figures with the accountant and occasionally an emergency may demand that the banker appoints an independent accountant to examine the borrower's books and business and to extract a balance sheet at a convenient date, with a special detailed report on the position. Such cases are, however, exceptional and outside the ambit of this review.

PRO FORMA BALANCE SHEET

In order to apply all the principles involved, the balance sheet of an imaginary company, XYZ Limited (see p. 43 and for easier reference end of book), has been compiled for the purpose of illustration and will be the main basis upon which the analysis will be developed. To facilitate calculation when the method of estimating risk is explained, a column has been provided for those who wish to assess their own opinion of the forced sale value of the various assets. The lessons to be learnt from this balance sheet of XYZ Limited as at April 30, 1978, will be brought out as the picture is painted.

METHOD OF APPROACH

There are two basic methods of banking approach to any balance sheet. They are *complementary and not alternative* and can conveniently be christened the *"going concern basis"* and the *"gone concern basis"*. Each will be described in detail later. It is enough to note that the going concern approach enables the banker to decide whether, from an interpretation of the figures revealed in the balance sheet, as amended by the expenditure of the required advance (plus the introduction of any fresh capital, etc., if any), the financial strength of the borrower justifies the accommodation. In short, is the business in a sufficiently healthy financial condition to warrant support from the bank? If not, and the current weaknesses cannot be repaired, there is little point in proceeding further. But where the current position is acceptable, the next check will be to assess the possible risk in the event of failure at some remote date through circumstances now unforeseen. This secondary, but complementary, approach involves an estimate of the dividend likely to be paid to the unsecured creditors in the event of bankruptcy, or liquidation, as the case may be. It helps to prove the initial assessment and provides a final guide to the risk in the worst possible event. It is neither conclusive nor irrefutable evidence, but merely a guide to be considered in relation to all the other circumstances of any proposal. As such, its worth should be neither decried nor over-valued, but much more of this later. It is sufficient here to state generally that the banker has to adopt the "going, gone" technique of auction parlance to obtain a reliable picture of any unsecured risk. Without such assessment, blind lending akin to speculation or gambling would result.

DEFINITIONS

The terms used to describe various balance sheet features unfortunately vary widely, and as there are so many schools of thought it is best to attempt to define at the outset the terms which will be used throughout this book. Instead of variety and complexity, it is preferable to limit the classes of assets and liabilities for the sake of simplicity, but some alternative and perhaps more searching descriptions are mentioned, where

XYZ Limited

Balance Sheet as at 30th April 1978

LIABILITIES	Author-ised £	Issued £	£	ASSETS	Cost £	Depre-ciation £	£
CAPITAL & RESERVES				Goodwill	5,000	—	5,000
5% Cum. Preference Stock	5,000	5,000					
Ordinary Stock	15,000	12,000		**FIXED ASSETS**			
			17,000	(F) Factory & Land	16,000	4,000	12,000
	20,000			Plant & Machinery	12,000	3,000	9,000
				Fixtures & Fittings	4,500	1,500	3,000
General Reserve		7,500		Motors	6,000	2,000	4,000
Profit and Loss Account		3,500	11,000				
					43,500	10,500	33,000
			28,000				
				Quoted Investments at			4,000
				cost (market value 30/4/78			
LOAN CAPITAL				£4,250) Trade Investment			
6,000 Mortgage Deben-				at cost		2,800	
tures of £1 each		6,000		Less: amounts written off		800	
Less: redeemed and cap-							2,000
able of being reissued		1,000					
			5,000				
Loan (secured by mort-				**FLOATING ASSETS**			
gage on factory)			5,000	Stock in hand (as valued			
Unsecured Loan			2,000	by directors)		16,000	
				Work-in-Progress		8,000	
			40,000				24,000
Provision for Taxation			4,200	Debtors		28,000	
Hire Purchase Creditors			2,000	Less: Reserve for Bad and			
Trade Creditors			29,000	Doubtful Debts		2,000	
Bank Overdraft			14,000				26,000
Dividend Payable			800	Cash in Hand			1,000
			90,000				90,000

AUDITOR'S CERTIFICATE
We have obtained all the information and explanations which to the best of our knowledge and belief were necessary for the purposes of our audit. In our opinion proper books of account have been kept by the Company so far as appears from our examination of those books. We have examined the Balance Sheet which is in agreement with the books of account and returns. In our opinion and to the best of our information and according to the explanations given us, the said Balance Sheet gives the information required by the Companies Acts 1948 and 1967, in the manner so required and, with the foregoing observation, gives a true and fair view of the state of the Company's affairs as at April 30, 1978.

(Signed)...

(Date)...

applicable, in brackets. These will not be used in this review.

An *asset* may be defined loosely as cash or something which can be converted into cash, and a *liability* as a debt due for payment at some time.

A *fixed asset* is one which is employed more or less permanently in the business as an agent of production. For example, a factory or plant and machinery, or motors, which are not produced or bought for sale in the ordinary course of business.

A *current* or *floating asset* is one which is acquired in order that it may be converted back into cash in the course of the normal business cycle.

Starting with cash which is used to buy stock and to cover labour costs to turn the stock into finished goods, which, in turn, are sold, the asset changes to debtors, and the circle is completed by the collection of cash from the debtors. All assets at any time within this circle are, for the purpose of the banker, current assets. (This definition includes such varying and more discerning terms as "liquid assets," "circulating assets," "quick assets," "floating assets," and "floating capital".)

A *fictitious asset* is any asset which cannot be brought within the above two categories. For example, goodwill, formation expenses, and an adverse balance on profit and loss account are fictitious assets ("intangible assets" is an alternative description).

Fixed capital includes, for the purpose of this study, not only the capital of the proprietors, plus reserves and other undistributed profits, but also all forms of long-term secured and unsecured finance in the shape of debentures, mortgages and fixed loans. (It can, of course, be divided into proprietors' capital and loan capital or fixed borrowing.)

Current liabilities comprise all debts at short-term arising in the usual course of business outside the generic term "fixed capital". These will normally include trade creditors, hire purchase creditors, bank overdraft, taxation due and reserved, dividends payable, amounts due to subsidiaries, etc. (sometimes described as "quick liabilities".)

Working capital is the surplus in the balance sheet of fixed capital over the total value of fixed assets, plus any fictitious assets. Alternatively, it is the excess of current assets over current liabilities, which gives the same result (also described as "circulating capital" or "liquid capital" or "floating capital" or "liquid surplus").

These terms will be applied to the balance sheet of XYZ Limited when considering the analysis from the "going concern" viewpoint.

Chapter V Balance Sheets

The Going Concern Basis

The banker must first decide whether the current financial and trading position of the potential borrower is sound enough to warrant the required accommodation, and to this end there are several simple tests which can be applied at the outset. The balance sheet and trading and profit and loss figures of the customer usually furnish sufficient evidence to enable the banker to assess the position in relation to the basic principles of lending. The method of approach will necessarily vary between bankers, but the following simple tests can quickly be made by the trained mind without need for any detailed analysis of the figures. If the going concern aspect is satisfactory, the bank is dealing with a healthy borrower whose needs can then be discussed fully and the risk assessed by a more exhaustive analysis of the balance sheet figures. On the other hand, if the going concern approach reveals weaknesses which are incapable of correction, there is little point in wasting time on further calculations. Although many of the tests are complementary and closely linked with each other, attempt will be made here for the sake of simplicity to treat each test as a separate feature.

STAKE OF PROPRIETORS

How much capital have the proprietors invested in the business and what relation does it bear to the amount required from the bank? These questions are promptly answered from the first glance at the balance sheet. The capital must be clearly set out therein, distinguishing in the case of a limited company between the rights of various shareholders and showing the authorised share capital as well as the share capital actually issued. Reserves accumulated by retention of profits in the business and any balance remaining on profit and loss account are then added to the capital, representing in total the stake which the proprietors have in their own venture. If a substantial reserve has been built up from past profits, it is an indication of prudent management. Instead of distributing profits up to the hilt, a proportion has been set aside wisely each year for future development and as a provision for lean years. If the profit and loss balance appears on the asset side of the balance sheet, the customer has incurred losses in the past and the warning to the bank is obvious. Capital has been lost. Why? The reason for the losses and the real prospects of recovery then demand full investigation.

So-called "capital" reserves are also seen and these, too, are part of the proprietorship resources. They can arise in a number of ways including a capital profit resulting from the sale of a fixed asset or the upward revaluation of property previously shown in the balance sheet at a figure below the current market value.

The capital in the business is reduced by the accumulated losses in profit and loss account. The reasoning is simple but the warning comes from the initial glance at the balance sheet figures. A quick survey shows whether the capital is reasonable in relation to the size of the business and the amount required from the bank. Further features follow automatically from this initial assessment, but next in order perhaps is the loan capital, if any.

LOAN CAPITAL—SECURED CREDITORS

In many cases the proprietors are unable themselves to contribute sufficient capital and have to resort to long term borrowing or mortgage finance. For the present purpose, all such long term borrowing may be looked upon as part of the capital resources of the business, admittedly only lent to the proprietors against security, but nevertheless available for a reasonably long period to finance, if need be, capital outlay and development. Any loan which is repayable upon demand or within less than say twelve months does not come within this category. It is fugitive money which may have to be repaid at any time and cannot be regarded for this purpose as the equivalent of capital.

The appearance of loan finance in the balance sheet provides the next warning to the banker. The customer has already borrowed from other sources. Why? How much has been borrowed, upon what terms and what security has been given to the lender? Clearly, all these points must be considered and questions asked to amplify the brief picture given in the balance sheet. In most instances the other lenders will have obtained security on the assets of the bank customer and, if the bank is to contemplate granting unsecured accommodation, the prior rights of such secured creditors naturally weaken the bank's position. Unless such outside borrowing is relatively small, a bank will not generally be disposed to grant unsecured facilities. It is impossible to lay down a definite rule because the financial strength and needs vary widely according to the type and size of the business. A large public company may have a substantial debenture issue and yet borrow unsecured from its banker. A small partnership may obtain temporary bank accommodation for stock purchases notwithstanding the private mortgage already created by the partners on the firm's office building. But normally the presence of secured creditors in the balance sheet limits the capacity of the customer to borrow from the bank without providing suitable security. The total and general nature of any secured creditors can usually be seen at a glance and their effect upon the

47

position from the banking standpoint quickly appreciated.

Where any liability of a limited company is secured otherwise than by operation of law on any assets of the company, the balance sheet must disclose that the liability is so secured, although it is not necessary to specify in the balance sheet the actual assets charged as security. Moreover, where a company has power to reissue debentures which have been redeemed, appropriate details must be given in the balance sheet. Thus, in the case of a limited company customer a clear picture of any secured borrowing will be evident from the balance sheet. With other trading concerns it is usual for the auditors to insist that a secured liability is disclosed as a separate item and not hidden by inclusion with the trade creditors or other unsecured liabilities.

The banker, therefore, examines the liabilities for secured creditors and considers their impact on the position from two angles. Firstly, their size and prior rights in relation to the proposed banking advance and, secondly, their contribution to the effective capital resources of the borrower. The detailed information required to complete the analysis and the means of obtaining it can be left for discussion later. At this stage a general view is sufficient to satisfy the going concern approach.

Applying the above principles to the balance sheet of XYZ Ltd., it will be seen that the pure capital resources of this company amount to £28,000, comprising in addition to the issued capital of £17,000, a general reserve of £7,500 and a balance of £3,500 outstanding in profit and loss account. The company has also borrowed long term £5,000 against mortgage debentures, and £5,000 by mortgage of its factory, so that its effective capital resources are £38,000. Enquiry reveals that the unsecured loan of £2,000 was recently obtained from a friend of the chairman of the company. As it is repayable by the company at one month's notice, it is not equivalent to capital but must be regarded as a current liability. The fixed capital of XYZ Ltd., is therefore £38,000, and the fixed capital of any type of bank customer can normally be calculated in similar fashion from the initial survey of the customer's latest balance sheet.

LIQUID POSITION

With very few exceptions, the fixed capital of any business should be sufficient to finance the acquisition of all the fixed assets, leaving a reasonable surplus available for working capital, thereby limiting the extent to which the business has to rely upon trade credit and day-to-day borrowing to carry its current assets. The liquid position of the borrower varies according to the extent of the surplus of fixed capital over fixed assets, or, in other words, according to the extent of the working capital. The next test, therefore, is to assess the working capital or liquid position of the company. The total amount invested in the fixed assets of any concern can usually be seen without difficulty; and modern accounting practice is of great assistance in this respect because the fixed assets are normally scheduled together, with appropriate sub-totals. The Companies Act, 1948, requires a limited company to distinguish between its fixed, current and fictitious assets and to show how the fixed assets are valued and the amount of depreciation written-off. A similar picture will usually be presented in the balance sheets of other trading units. Stray assets of a fixed or fictitious nature may, however, be set out apart from the main group of fixed assets, and it is always prudent to read through the entire assets before deciding how much fixed capital has been invested in fixed assets, and is not therefore available as working capital. In short, this test demands that the value of all asset items, other than those which are readily realisable in the ordinary course of the business of the potential borrower, should be classified as fixed assets in assessing the liquid position. Detailed calculations and the patient dissection of every item are not, however, necessary at this juncture. A general estimate or comparison is quite sufficient to disclose any inherent weakness.

Turning again to the balance sheet of XYZ Ltd., it will be seen that goodwill, plus the scheduled fixed assets, total £33,000, but £2,000 has also been swallowed up in trade investments. The total of fixed assets for this purpose is therefore £35,000. The value of the quoted investments can be ignored on the assumption that the shares are readily marketable and can be converted into cash as required. In point of fact they should be sold before resort to further borrowing. Thus, with fixed capital of £38,000, XYZ Ltd. has acquired fixed assets valued at £35,000, leaving a margin of only £3,000 available for working capital. This is a very small margin and it is obvious that the company has had to rely on extended credit to carry current assets worth £55,000. The same result can be obtained by comparison between the totals of the current assets and the current liabilities of the company, but the position cannot usually be seen so simply in this way, and demands more mental calculation with increased risk of error where the bank manager has to read a balance sheet just produced by a director who is discussing the requirements of the company. The current liabilities of XYZ Ltd. total £52,000, against current assets (including the quoted investments) worth £55,000, providing the same surplus of £3,000 representing working capital, but this is not so obvious from the balance sheet as the more simple comparison originally made between fixed capital and fixed assets.

The liquid position, or lack of it, disclosed in the balance sheet may be affected by a fresh bank advance and this possibility has next to be considered. If the bank money or any part of it is to be used directly or indirectly to finance the purchase of fixed assets, the total fixed assets of the borrower will increase without any corresponding increase in the fixed capital, and the working capital will be reduced by the amount so spent. For example, if XYZ Ltd. wished to borrow a further £5,000 from the bank to buy new machinery, the current liabilities of the company would increase by £5,000, but the fixed capital would remain unchanged at £38,000, against fixed assets increased by £5,000 to £40,000, making a deficiency of £2,000 in working capital. In short, the company requires more capital and from this standpoint alone is unlikely to be able to increase its bank borrowing.

The degree to which fixed capital is frozen in fixed assets necessarily varies according to the type of business. A company engaged in production usually requires expensive buildings, plant and machinery compared with the value of its current assets turning over in the production cycle, whilst a broker or factors of goods may rent an office and possess negligible fixed assets, using nearly all his capital and credit to carry stocks and debtors. Nevertheless, the principle remains that fixed capital should more than suffice to buy all the fixed assets. The greater the surplus available for working capital, the more liquid the position and the healthier the borrower from the banking standpoint. Whether any given surplus is sufficient to satisfy the banker's requirements must depend upon the business of the borrower and many attendant features which cannot be discussed in this simple review, but the dangers of lack of liquidity can be emphasised to advantage.

If all the initial fixed capital of any productive or retailing concern is spent on the acquisition of the fixed assets, it must rely upon short term borrowing and trade credit to finance purchases of goods and to cover labour costs and all overheads pending the collection from debtors of the proceeds of goods sold. This complete reliance upon credit at the outset is a serious weakness. Delay in the collection of debtors or a reduction in sales may not permit the prompt payment of trade creditors. Whilst profits as they accumulate will provide working capital to reduce the strain, and the payment of taxation due on the profits may be deferred, losses may instead be incurred in the early stages and the whole edifice will crumble if capital or loans cannot be obtained to meet pressing creditors. The dangers are greater where insufficient capital is available to acquire the fixed assets and the concern relies on hire purchase finance, deferred credit and short term loans to complete their purchase. Current liabilities should at least be covered by current assets, otherwise the risks of overtrading develop. The concern is trying to achieve too much on too little and any unexpected hitch in the smooth progress of production or the total of sales will soon precipitate a crisis, because there is no margin whatever available to meet the trade creditors. In the *pro forma* example, XYZ Ltd. is relying largely upon its heavy trade creditors and bank overdraft to carry its stocks and debtors. This may be dangerous.

The assessment of the liquid position of the borrower is therefore the vital test in the going concern approach to the balance sheet. It is impossible to lay down rules because each position has to be judged on its own merits, but the larger the surplus of fixed capital over fixed assets the healthier will be the financial strength of the borrower. An excess of fixed assets over fixed capital or the absence of working capital demands care and will normally indicate that any borrowing should be against approved security with adequate margin. In practice, it will be found that many smaller concerns suffer from lack of working capital, but advances can nevertheless be arranged on a satisfactory basis. Frequently it will be in the best interests of the customer to draw attention to the need for more capital and to decline to grant accommodation, however well it may appear to be secured, until he either brings in more capital or curtails the extent of his trading. The liquid position can sometimes be improved by the disposal of surplus fixed assets, or the arrangement of long term finance. On the other hand, it must not be forgotten that the liquid position deteriorates if losses are sustained, or excessive dividends are paid. Everything points to the need for liquidity if unsecured advances are to be considered.

GENERAL SUPPORTING TESTS

If the business of the potential borrower is conducted in a satisfactory manner, it will be meeting its liabilities promptly as they fall due, collecting all its receipts regularly and carrying just sufficient stock to meet normal needs. These features can easily be verified from the balance sheet figures and trading accounts.

If the total of trade creditors in the balance sheet is compared with the total purchases shown in the trading account for the year, a rough estimate can be made of the period of credit taken by the customer. Where the total creditors appear to be excessive in relation to purchases, enquiries should be instigated to find out why there has been such a delay in payment. For example, if the purchases made by XYZ Ltd. in the year to April 30, 1978 were shown in the trading account at £360,000, the amount of £29,000 outstanding at the balance sheet date is reasonable, representing about one month's credit. On purchases of only £120,000 the total of the creditors outstanding would be the equivalent of three months' credit, which normally would be excessive. In such event creditors may already be pressing.

Similarly, a comparison of the total debtors in the balance sheet with the sales figure for the trading period affords a simple guide to the speed of collection of debtors. If the customer from this calculation appears to be granting longer than normal trade credit, enquiries should be made. Perhaps the sales manager needs to increase pressure for collection, but there may be some debtors who are finding it difficult to meet their liability.

An unduly heavy stock held at the balance sheet date may indicate sales resistance or excessive stock piling beyond the capital resources of the customer. A rough check can be made by a comparison with the sales figure in the trading account. Is the stock on hand heavy compared with the normal sales? In a healthy business with satisfactory avenues of supply stocks will be kept to the minimum, but it may sometimes be necessary to take into account the incidence of seasonal fluctuations on some types of business.

This rough check made from a speedy initial survey of the figures serves its purpose in confirming or otherwise the current financial and trading health of the business. A more detailed analysis has to be made of all these items under the gone concern heading to be discussed in the ensuing chapters.

CONCLUSION

If this general survey of the balance sheet figures discloses that the capital resources of the borrower are adequate in relation to the amount required, whilst the liquid position is reasonable having regard to the type of business and there are no unduly large secured creditors ranking before the bank, there is ample evidence that the customer is credit-worthy. A final assessment from the gone concern aspect has then to be made to enable the banker to estimate the risk. But where the going concern approach reveals an unsatisfactory liquid position or casts doubts upon the current financial or trading health of the customer, there will be no need to explore the matter further.

Chapter VI Balance Sheets

The Gone Concern Approach (part 1)

THE FIXED ASSETS ANALYSED

If the banker is satisfied from a general survey of the balance sheet that the current financial position of the potential borrower is reasonably sound in relation to requirements, the next step may be to make a much more detailed analysis of the position, using what is known as the break-up or gone concern technique. Whether all the tests outlined in this and subsequent chapters are employed in every case will usually depend upon the relative importance, or perhaps marginal nature, of the advance and the practice of the particular bank, but all the major features have been included to present as complete a practical picture as possible. Even though a bank may not pursue the analyis to the point of actually estimating the final risk, many of the principles to be discussed will inevitably be applied to a survey of the assets disclosed in the balance sheet. What follows must not, therefore, be regarded as an inelastic, hidebound method to be employed in full regardless of the circumstances of any particular proposal. It is a description of the detailed tests available for adoption as the need arises. They are complementary to the going concern basis and, at best furnish a supplementary guide to the bank to assist in reaching the correct decision.

BASIC PRINCIPLES

This final approach is made on the assumption that the current financial position is strong enough to warrant granting the advance, but with the appreciation based on long experience that, through circumstances which cannot be foreseen, the borrower might fail at some indefinite and relatively remote future date. If the going concern approach to the balance sheet reveals the risk of failure within a short period, no advance will be granted or steps will be taken to curtail or to recover any existing indebtedness. The prospect will be apparent at a glance from the balance sheet figures. On the other hand, the strongest financial position can be irrevocably damaged by serious trading reverses, over-optimism, bad management, unexpected competition, changes in fashion, new inventions or even a general trade depression. What would be the position of the bank if any such unexpected development arose after the advance had been taken? The only safe test is to attempt to estimate the position on the worst possible basis, which must be the bankruptcy or liquidation of the borrower. In such event, however remote or unlikely it may appear to be at the time when the advance proposal is under consideration, the assets remaining would have to be sold by the agents of the trustee or liquidator under the hammer, in the worst possible conditions, to produce cash. After covering all the costs of winding-up, the proceeds of such forced realisation would then be distributed to meet the claims of the secured and preferential creditors, and lastly, if enough remained, to pay a dividend to the unsecured creditors. The object of the approach, therefore, is to estimate what dividend would be payable to the bank and other unsecured creditors in the event of the failure of the borrower in the remote future, and the method is first to assess the forced sale value of the assets according to the likely market available for them, and then to decide how the total cash proceeds would be distributed between the various creditors according to their respective rights.

It must here be emphasised that there can be no rule of thumb or standardised table of percentages applying to every case. Each balance sheet is an entirely separate problem demanding independent assessment of the assets according to their age, type and marketability, all of which vary with the nature of the business of the borrower. Bearing this warning in mind, the general points to be considered when assessing the forced sale value of typical assets can now be discussed with reference to the balance sheet of XYZ Ltd. With imagination, the reader can apply the principles to the assets shown in this balance sheet and estimate a break-up value for each of them, so tracing step by step this means of estimating risk. At the same time, other features of relative interest to the banker will be brought out concerning such typical assets.

GOODWILL

This intangible asset which so often appears in a balance sheet can never have a precise value. Goodwill was defined as long ago as 1810 as "the probability that old customers will resort to the old place". In fact it is the value attached to the reputation and connection of any business and in this respect may well be a real asset. It is perhaps primarily upon the admitted value of this asset that lending bankers regularly grant extensive facilities, but this does not mean that a large balance sheet figure for goodwill is a welcome feature. It is an asset to be sensed from experience of the customer rather than to be seen in the balance sheet, and little, if any, value can be attached to it from the break-up standpoint. No mention of such an asset appears in the balance sheets of our joint stock banks to-day, but obviously they must enjoy immense goodwill, constituting in effect a secret reserve. The balance sheets of many well known public companies likewise ignore goodwill as an asset or include it at a quite nominal value.

Goodwill, particularly in the case of a private trader, professional man, or a partnership, may originate from the personal reputation and influence of the owner or partners, or it may be built up on the quality of the goods sold or manufactured, or created by the situation of the business, enjoying perhaps local monopoly, or by judicious advertising—(We're with the Woolwich!). Sometimes such goodwill is valued and capitalised. The cost of an advertising campaign may be partly charged to goodwill account, or when a new partner is admitted to a firm the shares of the existing partners may be increased by the creation of goodwill which it is estimated they have built up before the new partner joins them. Frequently in the case of a limited company incorporated to acquire an existing business, goodwill represents the difference between the price paid for the business and the actual estimated value of the net assets. This excess price so paid is debited to goodwill and should bear a direct relation to the super profits of the business, being the profits remaining after all expenses, including reasonable remuneration for management, and the payment of the market yield on capital employed in a similar type of business.

Whatever may be the origin of any goodwill appearing in a balance sheet, the fact remains that it cannot have any value if the business fails. Successive bad years must reduce the goodwill and when the crash occurs it will be worthless. It follows that for break-up purposes the value of goodwill can be ignored.

This asset is normally disclosed as a separate item in every balance sheet and, in the case of a limited company, it must be set out under a separate heading. According to clause 8 (1) (b) of the Eighth Schedule of the Companies Act, 1948, if the amount of goodwill or part thereof is shown as a separate item in, or is otherwise ascertainable from the books of the company, or from any contract for the sale or purchase of any property to be acquired by the company, or from any documents in the possession of the company relating to the stamp duty payable in respect of any such contract, or the conveyance of any such property, the said amount so shown or ascertained so far as not written-off shall be shown under a separate heading. Precisely the same rules apply to any patents and trademarks included in the assets of a limited company.

PATENTS AND TRADEMARKS
The value of any patents and trademarks is likewise dependent upon the contined success of the business and can therefore best be ignored by the prudent bank lender. It would certainly be difficult to find a buyer for a patent when the concern owning it had failed. The goods produced under the patent were probably unmarketable and no one else is likely to wish to manufacture them. Exceptions can, of course, arise where the failure results from bad management or lack of capital. Incidentally, a patent is granted for a period of sixteen years so that in any event its value is reducing year by year, and depreciation should be written-off accordingly.

The registration of a trademark is also for sixteen years, but it may be renewed without undue difficulty.

To date no cash has been realised for the global fund of the imaginary liquidator or trustee, but an analysis of typical fixed assets may produce more tangible results.

THE FIXED ASSETS

A fixed asset has already been defined as one which is employed more or less permanently in a business as an agent of production and it has been agreed that in any financially healthy concern the cost of all the fixed assets should normally be found from capital resources. It is next necessary to decide which are the fixed assets in any balance sheet under review. The same type of asset may be a fixed asset in one balance sheet and a current asset in another balance sheet according to the nature of each business. For example, a ship in the course of construction on the stocks will be a current asset, part of the work-in-progress, in the balance sheet of the shipbuilder, but when it is launched and afloat at sea it will be a fixed asset in the balance sheet of the shipowners. Again, land and buildings are usually fixed assets, but in the figures of a builder engaged perhaps on estate development they will be part of his stock in trade. It is not usually difficult in practice to distinguish between a fixed and a current asset. Moreover, in most balance sheets to-day the assets will be found grouped under their appropriate headings. Clause 4 of the Eighth Schedule of the Companies Act, 1948, as amended under Clause 3 of the First Schedule of the Companies Act, 1967, demands that a limited company shall distinguish between its fixed, current or floating and other assets, classifying them under headings appropriate to the company's business, and the principle is often adopted by other business units.

In the event of failure, the fixed assets will usually be found intact, but the market available for their disposal will necessarily be limited. Furthermore, as a general principle, it must be recognised that when cash is short repairs and replacements will be postponed so that, taking the worst view, the fixed assets will usually be in a poor condition for sale by auction, when the need arises. From the banking standpoint, the best approach to the value of any asset, fixed or current, is to decide from the information available the answers to the following three questions raised in the given order:—

1. How is the asset valued in the balance sheet?
2. What is the current estimated worth of the asset?
3. How much is the asset likely to realise in the remote future if it has to be sold by auction in the worst possible conditions?

Once upon a time the balance sheet value of a fixed asset represented its worth to the business as a going concern, but with the inflationary experiences of the past decades many such assets acquired years ago may, in the absence of revaluation, still be valued at their original cost price, less depreciation, and appear in the balance sheet at a figure which is a mere fraction of their real worth to-day. Certain of the provisions of the 1967 Companies Act were designed to limit the occurrence of takeover bids which took advantage of undisclosed differences between balance sheet and market valuations of fixed assets. Directors are required to declare any major discrepancies in these valuations and to provide information on how and when the valuations were obtained. The date of purchase, the current valuation of fixed assets and the basis of this valuation must therefore be analysed in relation to the current price level. It is not *ultra vires* for a company to revalue any asset which has appreciated in value. In the absence of detailed information, the only prudent course will be to ignore any inflationary rise in value since the date of purchase or valuation to rely on the balance sheet figure as a basis for estimating the forced sale value. This method may obviously result in a gross under-estimate of the break-up value of the given asset to the detriment of the customer's proposal, but it is not always possible to collate reliable information on the current worth of every fixed asset. The borrower's views will naturally be optimistic, whilst the practical bank manager is not normally qualified to express an opinion concerning the value of the fixed assets of a manufacturing or kindred concern. Many factors have to be weighed in the balance and the more complete the information obtained from a study of the figures and from discussions with the customer the more accurate will be the final assessment. But it is not always feasible or desirable to pry into the details. In any event, pressure of business upon the bank may not permit of an exhaustive examination. Each case must therefore, be dealt with according to its merits. Where the advance is relatively large or the risk real, by reason of a vulnerable financial position, the bank will perhaps wish to analyse each asset in detail, but otherwise a more general estimate may suffice relying merely upon the quoted figures.

Where the balance sheet of a limited company is under review the method of arriving at the amount of any fixed asset will be clearly disclosed in keeping with Clause 5 of the Eighth Schedule of the Companies Act, 1948, as amended under Clause 10 of the First Schedule of the Companies Act, 1967. If possible, a limited company must show the cost price of the fixed asset, or if it stands in the books at a valuation the amount and date of that valuation and by whom made, the aggregate amount provided or written-off since the date of acquisition or valuation, as the case may be, for depreciation or diminution in value, the additions and disposals of property carried out by the company during the year, and a breakdown of the total under freehold, and long and other leasehold assets. For simplicity, only the bare essentials have been shown for XYZ Ltd.

The above general principles can now be applied to typical fixed assets.

LAND AND BUILDINGS

Many points have to be considered before determining the forced sale value of this asset, which is common to most balance sheets. What is actually included in this item? It may be perhaps a farm, a hotel, undeveloped land, a factory, a warehouse, office buildings, shops, a large emporium, or blocks of houses, a quarry, a hole in the ground, or a conglomeration of several of such buildings. Different methods of valuation clearly apply to such different types of property. A reasonable description of the chief properties and their situation is therefore the first requirement and, unless the properties are numerous and widespread, the best course will be for the local manager to inspect them and to describe and report upon them quite apart from the balance sheet. After all, if the properties are charged to the bank or offered as fresh security, full details will be required for record and valuation purposes. As a counsel of perfection, the same principles apply in valuing this asset in the balance sheet, even though the advance is to be unsecured or supported by collateral or other security. Admittedly, it may not always be practical or desirable to collate such a complete picture and in isolated cases only is the banker likely to call for a detailed schedule from a customer, such as a brewery, retailer, large scale manufacturer, or property owner with innumerable public houses, shops, factories, or office blocks, etc., as the case may be. In such circumstances a general view must usually be taken from the information in the balance sheet, and what follows is necessarily limited to cases where the borrower has only one or two main properties which can conveniently be considered apart from the balance sheet.

How much data is available at the outset? The 1967 Companies Act requires directors in their annual report to give more information on significant changes in the value of interest in land and buildings. Under Section 16(a) if the market value differs substantially from that shown in the balance sheet the attention of the shareholders of the company is to be drawn to the fact. This will normally be contained in a note to the balance sheet, which will also detail assets acquired during the year and a breakdown of leasehold and freehold properties. (Schedule 1 Companies Act 1967.) If the deeds of the property are held in safe custody, the date of purchase and the consideration can be ascertained therefrom. In the light of these facts, if they can be obtained, the next point perhaps is to consider the adequacy or otherwise of the amounts written-off by way of depreciation since the original purchase. Does the net figure for the asset in the balance sheet represent a reasonably prudent maximum value for the property to-day? How much is it likely to realise if it has to be sold in the indefinite future at auction to a small group of most unwilling buyers gathered together in the local hotel on a cold wet day? Before venturing an opinion on this point, the local manager will probably consider, *inter alia*, the following features according to the class of property under review.

In the case of a factory, its situation, size, age, and state of repair will first be considered. Is it a modern building with ample window space to provide natural light for the workers? Is it well-planned and suitable for many types of industry or capable of conversion without undue expense to meet the requirements of a buyer producing a different product? The ease, or otherwise, with which it might be converted to another use is an important factor. If the borrower fails, it may be that there is a surfeit of the supply of his goods in the market and a competitive producer is unlikely to require more factory space. Any potential buyers will, therefore, usually be engaged in a different business and they will consider the alternatives available to them. It may be cheaper and more satisfactory to buy virgin land and to erect a new factory thereon, planned to meet their precise needs, than to buy the existing factory and then to spend a considerable sum on alterations. The more adaptable the building the larger will be the market in the event of a forced sale, whilst the greatest difficulty will be experienced in finding a buyer for a specialised factory. Spacious bays and large areas of floor space can be adapted or divided as required with little expense, but it would be costly to break down a conglomeration of small rooms in a large factory building to provide space for mass production on a belt system. The situation of the factory has next to be considered in relation to rail and roads for transport of the raw materials inwards and the finished goods outwards. Its position in relation to the labour supply is also important. A factory sited in the middle of, or near to, housing areas has few labour difficulties, but where it is remote from the houses of the workers their transport presents a problem and may entail more running expenses than can be justified by the purchase of a factory at a lower price than one which could be bought in a populated region. The current transport and labour experiences of the customer will be a guide in this respect.

The site value may be material irrespective of the size, age and state of repair of the factory itself. The worth of the building may perhaps be rapidly depreciating owing to wear and tear, but the land on which it stands may be steadily appreciating in value for future development. All these, and probably other factors, have to be weighed in the balance to decide what market might be available in the event of the failure of the owner. The final estimate must from experience be based on the most pessimistic view. It is far safer to undervalue than to suffer in later years the penalties of undue optimism. In normal times it is surprisingly difficult to find a buyer for the more modern and well situated factory buildings, and the branch manager with little experience in such matters cannot expect to be accurate, particularly where he has to rely upon incomplete data. It follows that he must err freely on the side of caution and estimate a final figure which is beyond doubt the lowest which could be expected in the very worst possible conditions. It must be emphasised that the banker is not here attempting to assess the current worth of the factory. When available, a professional valuation is a useful guide, but it will usually quote the worth of the building at the given date if sold by treaty. The forced sale price in the event of trouble in the future will necessarily be much lower and prudence demands a heavy discount of the current value.

Precisely the same principles apply to other types of buildings, although the actual valuation may be based on different considerations. In the case of an hotel, its situation in relation to demand and local amenities will be important and its size will be quoted according to the number of bedrooms available for letting. Agricultural land will be valued according to its situation, acreage and quality, whilst office buildings or investment properties may be valued according to floor space and net yield, in addition to their state of repair and situation. It is impossible here to enter into a full description of the methods that can be adopted in valuing different types of properties. The point is that the land and buildings should, wherever possible, be considered apart from the balance sheet and valued for this purpose on a forced sale basis, erring always on the pessimistic side. If no details of the asset are available, an estimate has to be made from the information disclosed in the balance sheet, but the figure so taken clearly cannot be as reliable as one based on actual facts.

Having decided the value, two further points demand consideration. Firstly, are the buildings insured for at least the break-up value against the risk of loss by fire, etc? The bank may not be entitled to hold the policy, but it is prudent in many cases to verify the extent of the insurance cover. Secondly, it is necessary to determine whether the property or any part of it has been charged as security to any creditor. In the case of a limited company balance sheet, the initial warning will be evident from the note which has to be made against any liability of the company which is secured otherwise than by the operation of law, and the details can soon be ascertained by a search at the Companies Register. If the estimated break-up value exceeds the total secured liability, there will be a surplus available from the property for the preferential and unsecured creditors, but where the value is considered to be less than the amount owing to the secured creditor, the entire proceeds will be swallowed up and that creditor will rank *pari passu* with the other unsecured creditors for the balance unpaid. These principles apply to all assets which are charged in any fashion to secure liabilities. The reader is invited to assess the value of the freehold factory and land belonging to XYZ Ltd., attention being drawn to the fact that it has been mortgaged according to the balance sheet to secure a loan of £5,000.

PLANT AND MACHINERY

The next fixed asset which is common to manufacturing concerns will have much less value in the event of a forced sale because it is peculiar to the business under review. The possible market must be considered in relation to the general age and type of the machinery. It may have been heavily depreciated since the date of purchase, but the fact remains that, in these days of rapid progress, modern inventions and changed production methods may soon render plant valueless except as scrap. Moreover, the choice available to any buyer at auction must be considered. At best, if the machinery is up-to-date and in good repair, it will have to be taken down, transported to the buyer's place of business, and reassembled with considerable labour costs thus added to the purchase price. It may be cheaper to buy new machinery direct from the manufacturer, who will deliver and assemble it free of charge and often furnish a guarantee to cover the running of the plant for a limited period. The market for the second-hand machinery may be further limited because it is suitable only for the same type of business, and there will probably be a general depression in that trade when the customer fails. Estimates will no doubt vary according to the type of business of the borrower, but the above points suffice to show that the balance sheet figure must be heavily depreciated. The plant and machinery of XYZ Ltd. may well be worth £9,000 to the business as a going concern to-day, but it would be worth only a mere fraction of this figure if the company went into liquidation in say 1982. Probably, with cash shortages in the months and years prior to failure, the machinery will be in the poorest condition and will attract few buyers other than scrap merchants. This is the only safe method even though the customer may assure the banker that the plant to-day is worth much more than the balance sheet figure. It is important to remember that if the buildings are mortgaged any plant fixed to the premises is attached by the mortgagee. Another point to watch is whether any of the plant is subject to a hire purchase contract, in which case the hire purchase creditor will usually be entitled to the plant under the terms of the agreement where amounts remain unpaid.

LOOSE TOOLS
Sometimes this asset appears under a separate heading in the balance sheet. Loose tools are not often valued in the same way as other fixed assets, because depreciation by ordinary methods is impracticable. They will usually be valued by an official of the company and their forced sale value, whilst dependent to a certain extent on the factors which were considered above for machinery, will be much lower as they will probably be sold by auction in job lots. In fact, unless the item is comparatively large, it can prudently be ignored.

FIXTURES AND FITTINGS
However attractive and valuable the furniture and fittings may appear to

be to the lender when visiting the office or works of the customer, they can be worth little at auction if they have to be uprooted, carted away, altered, set-up and polished by the buyer. They will not fit another office without alteration and the expense of removal may be considerable. In short, they are worth very little when it comes to an alteration or sale of the premises. If the property is leasehold, some of the fixtures may become the property of the freeholder at the expiration of the lease. On the other hand, there is a much wider market for furniture, which is movable, and if the balance sheet under review is that of a hotel or kindred business and the furniture is known to be in good condition, the forced sale value will be proportionately higher.

In other words, comparatively little has been collected to date from the forced sale value of the assets other than from the property itself.

MOTORS

How much are the vehicles belonging to the customer likely to realise under the hammer in the event of failure in years to come? Will the supply of such motors then be much in excess of the demand for them? The basic principles of assessment are clear and prudence again demands pessimism. The following points have to be considered.

The age and type of the motors, and the depreciation already written off, will furnish an initial picture to enable the banker to decide whether the balance sheet figures are reasonable in relation to current second-hand values. If the cost of repair work during the past trading period is disclosed in the profit and loss account, it will provide a further guide to the condition of the vehicles. A fleet of cars for travellers will command a wider market in the event of a forced sale than a number of lorries specially constructed for the particular business. The delivery vans of a wholesale or manufacturing concern are likely to last longer and maintain their value better than vehicles used by a building contractor who has to drive them over rough land. The possible market for vehicles of the given age and type is important, but in any event a substantial deduction from the balance sheet value will usually be deemed prudent in making an estimate of the forced sale value. In any case, if funds are short, repairs will be cut to the minimum and replacements avoided, so that the lorries or motors will be in a much worse condition if and when the business fails. In short, the break-up value of the motors owned by XYZ Ltd. will be a mere fraction of their balance sheet figure of £4,000, whatever they may comprise in the imagination of the reader. Assuming for the sake of argument that there is only one motor, a Rover saloon purchased in 1976. It is probably well worth £4,000 to-day, but how much is it likely to realise in say 1982. Such reasoning has to be applied to all fixed assets under this heading.

INVESTMENTS

In the balance sheet of a trading concern, investments, other than in subsidiary companies, may be regarded as *quasi* fixed assets. They are neither retained as agents of production nor acquired in the usual course of business for conversion into cash in the course of the trading cycle. Usually, they represent surplus capital resources not required to finance current trading, and invested to produce income pending a demand for their proceeds in the business. It follows that where a customer who wishes to borrow produces a balance sheet disclosing relatively large quoted investments, the banker will first suggest that they should be realised to reduce the amount required on overdraft. On the other hand, where the borrowing is for quite temporary purposes, it may not be advisable to realise a sound investment, which may yield more than the overdraft will cost the customer. In such circumstances the investments will be available to the bank and most acceptable as marketable security. Whether they are retained for the time being, or sold to repay temporary bank accommodation, will depend entirely upon the detailed facts, but the basic principles are clear.

The next point is to ascertain the nature of the investments and the way in which they have been valued. A limited company is required by Clause 8 of the Eighth Schedule of the Companies Act, 1948, as amended by Clause 9 of the First Schedule of the Companies Act, 1967, to disclose in its balance sheet under separate headings the aggregate amount respectively of the company's quoted and unquoted investments. Moreover, quoted investments have to be subdivided where necessary to distinguish between those which have and those which have not been granted a quotation or permission to deal on a recognised stock exchange. Where the aggregate market value of the quoted investments of a company differs from the amount of the investments stated in the balance sheet, a note has to be added revealing the market value. (See the figures for XYZ Ltd.) Finally, it is worthy of note that a limited company has to disclose separately in its profit and loss account the amount of income received from investments, distinguishing between quoted and unquoted investments. This information may enable the banker to calculate the average yield on the investments shown in the balance sheet. In the case of a limited company, therefore, its balance sheet will disclose all the essential information required to decide the worth of such assets from the banking standpoint. With other customers, enquiry may be necessary to interpret the investment item and a schedule of investments requested for valuation purposes.

Where a list of the investments is supplied by the customer they can easily be valued at current prices and the appropriate margin deducted according to the nature of the holdings. If such details are not forthcoming, but the shares are known to be marketable, an adequate margin can be allowed on the given market value to cover the risk that speculative stocks may be included in the total. If there has been a general fall in market prices since the date of the balance sheet, a further allowance may be necessary. In the absence of reliable information concerning any of the investments, prudence dictates that their value should be ignored.

Quoted shares normally present little difficulty, but unquoted shares and trade investments are in a different category. Adequate information is rarely available to determine their value with any degree of accuracy, and their market for sale is often hedged with restrictions. The attitude of the banker will depend upon the amount locked up in such investments in relation to the total assets of the customer. Usually, the amount is relatively small and the item may be ignored. Where it is of sufficient importance, the banker may ask to see the latest audited balance sheet of the company or companies concerned so that the worth of the shares can be estimated from an analysis of such figures. Alternatively, a cautious estimate of their value may be based on the average yield from the shares over a few years compared with the average market yield on quoted shares of a similar type of business. These methods of valuation of unquoted shares from balance sheet figures can best be left for consideration until the completion of the explanation of the principles of break-up.

SHARES IN SUBSIDIARY COMPANIES

Nowadays this item frequently appears in the balance sheet of a limited company customer. It is undoubtedly a fixed asset, very difficult to realise and of doubtful value unless adequate information is forthcoming to enable the banker to make a reliable estimate.

Where any limited company holds more than half in nominal value of the equity share capital of another company, or as a member of another company controls the composition of its board of directors, then the other company is a subsidiary. The mother company with the majority interest in the subsidiary is known as the holding company. Except where, in the opinion of the directors of the holding company, there are good reasons against it, the financial year of all subsidiaries has to coincide with the financial year of the holding company. A company with subsidiaries is required to produce group accounts disclosing the position and profit or loss of the holding company and of each of its subsidiaries. These include a consolidated balance sheet and a consolidated profit and loss account, combining the position of the holding company with that of the subsidiaries and showing separately the interest of any minority shareholders. Whilst this consolidated balance sheet serves to show the strength of the group, it is of little value otherwise to the banker who is lending to one of the companies in the group. In the event of the collapse of the group, each company would be wound-up quite separately, so that from the gone concern aspect the banker is primarily interested in assessing only the worth of any amounts due to a holding company from its subsidiaries, or *vice versa*, and the value, if any, of shares held in subsidiaries. To achieve this it is necessary to analyse the balance sheet of each individual company in the group.

Firstly, the link between the holding company and its subsidiaries has to be considered. The closer that link the more dependent the companies are upon each other, and the greater will be the risk of the collapse of the group in the event of the failure of any one company. If in fact they trade to a marked extent between themselves, each playing perhaps an essential part in the production of goods marketed by the holding company, the fortunes of the group will usually rise and fall together, but in many cases a subsidiary may operate and trade quite distinct from the holding company, whose majority interest is in the nature of an investment rather than a trade connection. In general, the closer the trading link between the holding and the subsidiary company, the more pessimistic will be the outlook of the banker estimating the worth of the holding company's interests in the subsidiary. Sometimes a holding company may itself be a subsidiary of another company, in which event there is a happy family group comprising perhaps a grandfather company, its subsidiary, the father company, and all its children. The complications of cross entries and set-offs between the members of such a family in order to value, say the interests of the grandfather company in the father company, can well be imagined if an attempt is made to analyse all the balance sheets of the members of the group.

The inter-company interests have to be revealed in the balance sheets of both the holding company and the subsidiaries. The holding company, according to Part II of the Eighth Schedule of the Companies Act, 1948, must disclose the amount of its assets consisting of shares in subsidiaries, and show separately the amounts owing, whether on loan account or otherwise, from or to the subsidiaries. In the balance sheet of any holding company, there will thus usually be three items distinct from the other assets and liabilities of the company.

1. Shares in subsidiaries.
2. Amounts due to the company from its subsidiaries.
3. Amounts due from the company to its subsidiaries.

The first two assets can be valued in the same way, although the shares are a fixed asset of the holding company, whilst the amounts due from the subsidiaries, unless on account of a long term loan, will be a floating asset, representing monies due for current inter-company trading activities.

The method of valuation is the same in principle as that now under discussion for any balance sheet viewed from the gone concern angle. If all the assets of the subsidiary are analysed and their worth assessed on the assumption that liquidation may occur in the indefinite future and the cash total representing the estimated proceeds is applied first in payment of all the secured and preferential liabilities, any surplus will be available to meet the unsecured creditors, including the holding company which will rank *pari passu* with other trade and unsecured creditors, and take a dividend in the normal way if there is not enough to pay 100p in the £. In such event, the worth of the floating asset described as amounts due from that subsidiary is ascertained and the shares held in the subsidiary are valueless. On the other hand, if there is an estimated surplus after payment of all the creditors (and any preference shares), it will be available for the shareholders, and the holding company's interests will be valued according to the proportion it holds of the total ordinary share capital of the subsidiary. Perhaps the following example will serve to clarify the principle.

Southtown Bank have the account of X Ltd. This company wishes to borrow unsecured and produces a balance sheet which reveals that it holds shares valued at £20,000 in a subsidiary, Z Ltd. In addition, there is £15,000 due by Z Ltd., to X Ltd., but nothing owing by X Ltd. to Z Ltd. The facts are clear from the balance sheet and a search at the Companies Register against Z Ltd. reveals that its issued share capital comprises £15,000, 6 per cent. preference shares, all held privately, and £30,000 ordinary stock, of which £20,000 is held by X Ltd. In response to the request of the bank, the directors of X Ltd. produce the latest audited balance sheet of the subsidiary, Z Ltd., and this is analysed on gone concern lines. It is estimated that the assets would produce upon a forced sale £100,000. Total creditors of Z Ltd. amount to £76,000, so they will all be paid in full and the item of £15,000 in the balance sheet of X Ltd., being monies due from Z Ltd., is therefore worth its face value. There is a surplus of £24,000 remaining after settling the claims of all creditors, but £15,000 of this is taken by the preference shareholders possessed of prior rights to the ordinary shareholders in the event of liquidation. Thus £9,000 remains for the equity capital, of which £20,000 out of £30,000 issued, or two-thirds thereof, is owned by X Ltd. It follows that the item "shares in subsidiary £20,000" in the balance sheet of X Ltd. is worth, from this standpoint, £6,000. The minority shareholders take the remaining surplus of £3,000. Many subsidiaries to-day are wholly owned by the holding company and it is therefore convenient to adopt the view that any surplus remaining after payment of all outside creditors will be available to the parent concern.

Whether the banker thinks it necessary to indulge in such a detailed analysis of subsidiary company balance sheets in order to estimate the value of the interests which the holding company customer has in its subsidiaries will naturally depend upon the extent of those interests in relation to the other assets of the borrowing company. Where the holding company is essentially an investment company, it will usually be preferable to lend direct to the subsidiary or subsidiaries which actually need the temporary accommodation and have the trading assets to support the proposal. In other cases where the holding company is the main productive unit, the interests in subsidiaries may perhaps be ignored or assessed at a prudent nominal value without resort to complicated calculations which, at best, are only remote estimates. In other words, the method must suit the case under review, instead of slavishly following a standard system regardless of the main point at issue. The foregoing paragraphs, however, describe the methods available to the banker if it is considered desirable and necessary to value the interests which a holding company borrower may have in subsidiary companies. They are all separate legal entities and the loan will be the liability of the borrowing company and not that of the group.

LOANS TO DIRECTORS (OR PROPRIETORS)

Section 190 of the Companies Act, 1948, as amended by Section 2 of the Companies Act, 1967, made it unlawful for any company to grant a loan to a director. There are very limited exceptions which can be ignored here, but where the asset does appear it may conveniently be regarded from the banking standpoint as a fixed asset, because its likelihood of speedy repayment will usually be remote. Where any advances have been made to directors or officers of a company, such loans must be disclosed separately in the balance sheet, in aggregate, together with any loans made or repaid during the period since the last balance sheet (Section 197). Thus any borrowing by directors cannot be hidden from the shareholders of the company. The only exceptions to this duty of disclosure are loans not exceeding £2,000 made by a company to any employee in accordance with a special scheme for the staff, and loans made in the ordinary course of business by a company, whose normal business includes lending money (*e.g.*, a bank). The balance sheet of a limited company, therefore, will reveal the position clearly and the first query from the banking standpoint will surely be that the company has lent surplus funds to directors yet it now requires to borrow from the bank. The reason for this policy may demand analysis according to the extent of the loan to the directors, who may well be unable to repay their debt. Perhaps they were unable to obtain financial assistance from other sources and the alleged floating asset of the company is in reality frozen.

For break-up purposes, the value of such loans will naturally depend upon the known financial standing of the director or directors concerned. Their names will not usually be disclosed in the balance sheet, but where the amount is material details should be obtained, and, if they are already borrowing from the bank on personal account or if they are guaranteeing the company's overdraft, their financial position may need to be closely watched. If they are customers of another bank, discreet enquiries may be thought necessary. Unless the directors are of undoubted financial standing with adequate resources outside the company itself, this type of asset can have little value from the gone concern standpoint. It may even discourage the banker from lending to the company in case further funds are diverted into loans to directors.

This concludes the survey of the typical assets which may be regarded as fixed assets from the banking standpoint. It is helpful to sub-total the forced sale values at this stage so as to see at a glance the minimum amount which such assets are estimated to realise in the event of failure. They will certainly be there upon liquidation or bankruptcy, but with cash shortages in previous months or years they will be in a poor condition, with repairs neglected and renewals deferred. Moreover, they are unlikely to command a wide market and may even be impossible to sell except as scrap. The drastic reduction which is usually made in the value of each item may at first appear to be extreme, but it is hoped that the reader will now realise the need for prudent pessimism in the light of past costly experience.

The Gone Concern Approach (part 2)

THE CURRENT ASSETS ANALYSED

For this purpose, a current asset has been defined as one which is acquired by any business in order that it may be converted into cash in the course of the normal trading cycle. In the case of a temporary trade advance, the bank debt will usually be repaid from the current assets as they are turned over in the course of the business. In the event of failure of the business, the current assets will generally be easier to realise or collect than the fixed assets, but when cash is short they will perhaps be much reduced in total before the final collapse. The proceeds obtained from sales during the final trading period, or from forced realisations, will usually be used to meet pressing creditors. Their importance naturally varies according to the type of business under review, but they will normally command closer attention from the lending banker than the fixed assets. The chief points of interest and the principles involved in considering such assets are outlined below.

GENERAL PRINCIPLES—STOCK

The first current asset is common to all balance sheets of trading customers and must be subject to many banking tests. How is it valued and what does the item include? It is not the auditor's duty to take stock or to verify its value, and there is rarely any independent outside check of the item as it appears in the trading account and balance sheet. While the auditor may perhaps advise upon the best method of valuation, he cannot be expected to make a physical check of any inventory. Stocktaking is a matter for the staff of the business who will therefore calculate its value according to a given formula. Some stocks are taken by specialists. For example, it needs considerable experience to take stock in an hotel bar or public house. In the case of a limited company, the value of the stock will be certified by the directors and the figures accepted by the auditors. In the case of a partnership, or private trader, the partners or the pro-prietor will be responsible for the stock valuation for the balance sheet. Thus the banker has to rely on the integrity and ability of the personal borrowers, or of the directors of a limited company, to reach a prudent and true valuation of stock in hand. The over-valuation of stock (and of work-in-progress—see later) can seriously distort the trading picture by inflating profits or hiding losses, and dishonest or imprudent customers can keep a business in being for a time by deliberately writing-up the value of its stocks. On the other hand, the deliberate under-valuation of stock reduces profits and creates a hidden reserve for the future. This practice may be adopted in good years in an attempt to limit a heavy tax liability arising from the real profits which were earned, but the banker naturally cannot make any allowance in his own calculations for any alleged under-valuation. All contentions that the stock is really worth much more than the balance sheet figure have, therefore, to be ignored, but the risk of over-valuation must not be forgotten, particularly in smaller concerns where a rough sight check of stock may be feasible. It follows that undue swings in the value of the stock from balance sheet to balance sheet call for inquiry. Normally, the banker is content to rely upon the integrity and experience of the customer to produce correct stock figures. An investigation by an independent expert acting for the bank is a very rare need.

There is an old accounting adage which demands that provision should be made for all possible losses and realised profits only taken into account. To comply with this principle, stock is usually valued at cost or market price, whichever is the lower. The only exceptions to this unwritten rule are stocks which undoubtedly increase in value with the passage of time, such as wine and certain types of timber. Thus any increase in the market value of stock is ignored and the price originally paid is the basis for the balance sheet valuation. On the other hand, if the market price has fallen since the date of purchase, then such depreciation in value has to be covered and the market price is the correct standard to adopt. In some types of business it may be difficult to follow this rule implicitly, but however onerous the task may appear to be to the proprietor, it is unwise to deviate far from it, and the prudent bank manager will rightly criticise any serious known shortcomings of a customer in this respect. For example, a retailer of innumerable lines may think it wasteful to maintain detailed records of the cost and market prices of all the goods in stock. Sometimes the current market price may be doubtful because the goods in question are no longer available in the wholesale market. In such event, unless they have a real scarcity value, they may be difficult to sell and their value in the balance sheet should be heavily written down, if not wiped-off entirely. In a well managed business, however, stock will normally appear in the balance sheet at cost price or market price, whichever is the lower with full provision for unsaleable or out-of-date items.

An omnibus stock item may include different categories of stock according to the nature of the business. Apart from perhaps packing materials (bags, wrapping-paper and twine), a retailer's stock will consist entirely of finished goods ready for sale to the consumer, but the stock item in the balance sheet of a manufacturer will usually include raw materials, work-in-progress and finished goods. In some cases there may also be by-products available for sale in a restricted market. If the position so demands, the banker may call for details, breaking down the stock figure under these main headings because the potential forced sale market for each category will be quite different.

INITIAL TESTS

If stock can be bought and delivered without undue delays, a healthy business will carry only sufficient stock to meet normal trade demands. The first test, therefore, is to ensure that the stock-on-hand is not excessive for the usual business requirements of the customer. The rate of stock turnover varies according to the type of business, but the banker should know the general trading conditions applicable to every customer and be able to decide whether the stock position is reasonable. In the case of a retailer or wholesaler, there will be accepted speeds of turnover with each line of goods sold. A provision merchant or fruiterer obviously turns over perishable stocks at weekly intervals, whereas a furrier or silversmith expects to hold stocks for several months. With a manufacturer the average time taken to convert raw materials into finished goods will be known and the stock figure can be checked roughly in relation to this cycle. A comparison of stock-on-hand with total sales in the year shows roughly how much stock is held to meet a given period of standard sales. If it appears to be excessive, enquiries should be made. An unduly high stock figure may mean that the customer is stockpiling in the hope of a rise in price or in preparation for a large increase in demand. This may or may not be an acceptable policy having regard to his working capital resources. On the other hand, an excessive stock-on-hand may result from bad buying and the accumulation of stocks which cannot be sold. The time to query the position is before the advance is granted or renewed. Where desirable, the speed of stock turnover in a business can often be compared with that of another customer in the same line of business. The quicker the turnover, the less likelihood of an accumulation of unsaleable items. In all cases, of course, regard must be had to any seasonable factors affecting the business. The stock of a specialist Christmas card manufacturer will clearly vary with the time of the year.

The next prudent test is to verify that the stock is fully covered by insurance against fire, theft and other known risks. Such insurance must be sufficient to cover the peak stock figure, otherwise the usual average clause will mean loss to the customer in the event of a partial loss. If the stock or part of it is pledged to the bank as security or if it is caught by a floating charge created by a limited company borrower in favour of the bank, this insurance question is of greater importance. In any event, the main source of repayment in the ordinary course of business is from the sale of stock and the whole stream will dry up if uninsured or under-insured stock is lost in a serious fire. An experienced customer is hardly likely to be careless in matters of insurance, but smaller retailers and others absorbed in the problems of production may lose sight of the fact that prices have risen and they are now often carrying stock in excess of the amount of their insurance cover. A prudent enquiry from the branch manager at an interview will not therefore be out of place.

If these features appear to be reasonable for the business under review, the gone concern aspect next calls for a consideration of the possible market available in the event of a forced sale. This can obviously vary to a marked extent according to the type of stock.

RAW MATERIALS

Raw materials will be included in the stock item of manufacturing and processing customers and in the balance sheets of brokers and suppliers dealing in such goods. They will normally be easier to sell than finished goods because they command a wider market. Some materials, such as cotton or wool, can be sold by description throughout the world, and can thus be realised without appreciable loss. A small allowance for possible market depreciation is therefore all that will be necessary in estimating the break-up value. Other raw materials may have relatively little value until they are processed into finished goods. In some cases the finished stock of one industry becomes the raw material of another industry in the trade process towards the finished goods marketed to the final consumer. For example, a cotton frock passes through several industries before it appears in the shop window of the retailer. The raw material is spun by one company and its product becomes the raw material for the weaver. It is then perhaps passed on as raw material for the dyer and finisher before it is sold to the merchant as his raw material for making-up into the finished frock. Clearly, the market for such raw material narrows as it passes to each stage. There will be innumerable buyers for the raw cotton of standard description, but the demand for cloth of a particular colour and design must be much more limited. Again, a manufacturer may be dependent upon a steady flow of many different raw materials which go into his final product in certain proportions. A delay or stoppage in the supply of any one of these components may hold up production, but from the other side of the picture the manufacturer may be a monopoly buyer of one of these raw materials and his failure will make the stock of the producer of that material virtually unsaleable. Suppose X Ltd. produces special transistors for Y Ltd., who manufacture computers. The transistors are finished goods in the balance sheet of X Ltd., but raw material components in the balance sheet of Y Ltd. Should X Ltd. fail, the market for the sale of their stocks is restricted entirely to Y Ltd., who may for some reason have ceased production of that particular product. The transistors are, therefore, unsaleable unless they have some scrap value. In other words, the banker must know the business of the customer, appreciate the nature of the raw materials, and assess the extent of the market available to absorb such stock should it be necessary to dispose of it under forced sale conditions. The narrower the market, the greater will be the depreciation of the balance sheet value of the raw materials.

FINISHED GOODS

The same principles apply to finished goods, but the problem is usually more simple. The type of goods, their speed of turnover, and elasticity of demand will soon enable the banker to estimate the market available in case of need. It is dangerous to draw general conclusions, but the failure of any seller of finished goods will usually result from his inability to sell those goods in sufficient quantities at reasonable profit. Such stock remaining on hand upon bankruptcy or liquidation cannot, therefore, be expected to sell comfortably at anything approaching its balance sheet value. Moreover, in the running down period, stock is unlikely to be replaced as it is sold, the proceeds being diverted to meet perhaps wages or pressing creditors. A material reduction of the face value set out in the balance sheet will therefore be prudent.

Everything depends on the nature of the goods and the possible market for a quick sale. The stock of a retail tobacconist, grocer or chemist will not require heavy depreciation in estimating its break-up value unless it is known to be cluttered up with luxury lines in doubtful demand. The stock of a store with rapid turnover and regular bargain sales can be valued comparatively higher than the stock of a retail draper with relatively slow turnover, and a pronounced tendency to accumulate unsaleable goods. The incidence of fashion or other possible changes in public taste must be borne in mind, particularly where the stock is in the luxury class. The policy of the customer in clearing out old-fashioned lines should be known, otherwise the stock may include items which have been in the business for years and are virtually unsaleable. If the banker is familiar with the customer's business and bears in mind the low prices usually obtained for surplus stocks sold under the hammer to unwilling buyers, it will not be difficult to estimate the market and fix a prudent figure for the stock from the gone concern standpoint, after due allowance for the costs of the auction, etc.

WORK IN PROGRESS

This item can be conveniently discussed under the heading of stock. When dealing with a manufacturing concern, it comprises the value of raw materials, plus labour expended thereon to bring them some way towards finished goods. The market for a forced sale is obviously narrow and work-in-progress may be unsaleable unless and until it can be completed. The length of the normal production cycle is, therefore, important. If raw materials are quickly turned into finished goods, a liquidator or trustee in bankruptcy may be prepared to complete the manufacture of all work-in-progress before stopping production, so that he can then sell the finished goods. On the other hand, if the manufacture and assembly stages occupy many months with correspondingly heavy labour costs, the machines may be stopped and the work-in-progress sold for what it will fetch. In such cases it is unlikely that competitive producers will wish to buy half-finished goods and the available market may be limited to their scrap content. Care is therefore necessary to ensure that the amount of work-in-progress does not become unduly large in comparison with the other floating assets of the business. There may be a clog in the wheels of production or some bottleneck which is suspect to the lending banker.

The item is of much greater importance in the balance sheet of a shipbuilder, building contractor and other types of large-scale constructors, whose main floating asset will be work in course requiring relatively large labour costs in relation to the raw materials employed. Moreover, this type of business is more prone to attempt too much in relation to its capital resources and the value of the work-in-progress will call for close analysis. The nature of the work will be known to the banker and the main contracts included therein should be considered. A break-down through failure before completion of a contract may entail heavy penalties. In any event, the contract will be of little worth unless and until it is completed, and a high price may have to be paid to competitive contractors to persuade them to complete it. Bad costing may mean that contracts in course are conducted at a loss, whilst the true position can remain hidden by over-valuation of the work done. The banker should, therefore, approach the item in a systematic manner.

The first need is to ascertain the main contracts included in the work-in-progress and to decide whether they are reasonable in relation to the experience and working capital resources of the customer. Is there already a danger that he is attempting too much? If so, a word of caution will not be out of place. Are the contracts subject to heavy penalties if they are not completed within a stated time? Are they fixed price contracts, or are the risks of increased costs in labour and raw materials suitably covered over the contract period? In the light of this information the banker can consider the prospects of the successful completion of the contract by the customer and appreciate what would happen if failure occurred before completion.

Secondly, it is important to find out how the work-in-progress has been valued. The customer may receive regular progress payments for work done. These may be subject to certain retentions (deductions from the contract price for the work done) payable only after completion of the entire contract and the passage of a stated time for testing the efficacy of the work. As such retention moneys accumulate they naturally reduce the cash resources of the contractor, particularly where they include more than the profit earned on the contract. How, therefore, are these features revealed and the work-in-progress valued in the balance sheet? Amounts received on account by way of progress payments should be deducted from work-in-progress and retentions should be disclosed as an item apart from trade debtors, because they will not be collected unless the contract is completed to the satisfaction of the employer or purchaser. They are a special class of debtor. At what stage work-in-progress is transferred to trade debtors is also of importance, as any hasty removal to debtors at a figure including all profit may distort the true position. But a lengthy construction job with heavy labour costs cannot always be carried to completion without some payment on account. The method of valuation of work-in-progress after deduction of all instalments received for work done to date is of vital importance. If the balance sheet figure includes all estimated profit on such work, without thought of any reserve for contingencies, there is the obvious risk of over-valuation, but some element of profit has to be included otherwise with long-term contracts spread over several years the customer would record large profits in the years when the contracts were finished and small profits or even losses in the years whilst they were in course. Unless the completion dates of the contracts were evenly spread over the years, the profit record of the concern would be very spasmodic with consequent tax complications. Some element of profit will therefore be included in the valuation of work-in-progress in the balance sheet of a large-scale contractor and must be taken into account by the banker in making an estimate of the gone concern value.

Having decided whether the item is prudently valued by the customer in the balance sheet, and knowing the essential facts to enable it to appreciate what penalties might be incurred and the difficulties which would face a receiver, liquidator, or trustee in bankruptcy, who would perforce have to try to complete the contracts, the bank will be able to estimate the value of the item. Clearly these tests are of greater value from the going concern basis because they will reveal whether the potential borrower really justifies acceptance of the risk entailed in granting the required advance.

TRADE DEBTORS

This next item is present in every balance sheet, unless sales are entirely for cash, and represents the total amount owing by those who have purchased goods or services from the business. The real value of the trade debtors naturally depends upon the ability of the debtors to meet their commitments, and in a well managed concern they should be nearly equivalent to cash. The number and type of debtors making up the balance sheet total is most important. The item will usually be large in relation to other assets and should be analysed with care. In some cases loans made by the business may be included under the general heading of sundry debtors, but, where known, they should be segregated and treated independently according to the financial standing of the borrower. The following tests apply to the pure trade debtors.

The initial comparison made between the total sales revealed in the trading account and the amount of trade debtors outstanding in the balance sheet will give a general idea of the length of credit granted by the customer. If debtors are large in comparison with total sales, it is an indication of slow payment for goods sold or work done, unless seasonal factors have to be taken into account. Is this grant of long-term credit necessary in the particular trade or is it prudent to advise the customer to exert pressure upon his debtors for speedier settlement? What has been the experience of the business in the past in collecting from debtors? The total bad debts written-off in the profit and loss account should be compared with the sales figure, preferably over several years, to get some idea of the customer's experience in this respect. A relatively large annual total of bad debts may indicate that the customer is slack in granting credit and a tactful word from the banker, with suitable reference to the status enquiry service, may result in greater care being exercised in the future. It may next be necessary to enquire the policy of the borrower in dealing with bad or doubtful debts. Are all bad debts promptly written-off and is a reasonable provision made for doubtful debts each trading year? Some concerns allocate a sum equal to a small percentage of the total debtors to a bad debts provision, whilst others examine their ledgers and pick out the doubtful debts to be provided for in the profit and loss account. Whatever system may apply, the banker will wish to be satisfied that the amount deducted from total debtors represents a reasonable provision, in the light of past experience and according to the number and type of the debtors, to cover all bad or doubtful items. Even the net figure after deducting this reserve cannot be accepted at its face value.

The next points to be explored will be the number and nature of the debtors. The larger the number of debtors comprising the total revealed in the balance sheet, the greater will be the spread of the risk and the smaller the prospect of loss. If the amount of £26,000 due to XYZ Ltd. is owing by, say, 520 customers of the company, the average amount due is only £50, but suppose £18,000 out of the £26,000 was due from A.B.C. Ltd. The failure of the latter company would unquestionably jeopardise the financial strength of XYZ Ltd., and, where relatively large amounts are found to be due from a few debtors, their financial standing may have to be closely considered. Whenever possible, a list of the chief debtors should be obtained to ensure that the total is well spread amongst many. Any unduly large debtors may be subject to enquiry.

The nature of the debtors is likewise of great importance. There is obviously a vast difference between the financial reliability of the credit customers of a fashionable dress shop granting long-term credit to attract buyers of expensive gowns, and the debtors of a printer who concentrates on the supply of cheque books and forms to banks and insurance houses. The type of business conducted by the customer will guide the banker in deciding what proportion of the total debtors may safely be regarded as good in the event of failure. A list of the main debtors will reveal the names and trade standing of those who normally buy from the customer. There may be foreign debtors included in the total and their ability to pay may have to be considered, together with any exchange restrictions which may have been imposed and the currency in which payments is to be effected. If foreign debtors are, to the bank's knowledge, insured with the Export Credits Guarantee Department, the risk is probably limited to the normal balance of 15 per cent. uncovered by such contracts. Sometimes a customer may sell entirely to Government departments or to local authorities and, although it may take longer to collect payments from such debtors, they can be looked upon as undoubted. There may even be a right of set-off available to a debtor who has also sold his goods to the customer and so appears in the total of trade creditors shown in the balance sheet. In such event, the set-off will discharge that creditor in full before the bank and produce no cash for the common fund. Moreover, if it should prove necessary to demand payment from debtors in order to wind-up a business, the total amount due may be reduced by discounts claimable in accordance with the terms of the particular trade.

The attitude of the banker will depend upon the extent of his knowledge of the debtors. Normally, if there is an adequate reserve for doubtful debts and the net total is reasonable in relation to annual sales, a relatively small reduction will suffice to reach an estimate of the amount likely to be collected by a receiver or liquidator. For obvious reasons a larger allowance will be advisable where the debtors have bought the goods on hire-purchase terms. The quality of the debtors is much more important than their book value.

When analysing the balance sheet of a builder or contractor, the likelihood that retentions have been included in the global trade debtors figure must not be overlooked. Such moneys will be retained by the debtors concerned under the terms of their contracts until they know from tests and experience that the work has been completed to their satisfaction. These retentions are in fact reserves retained to cover latent defects which may be discovered after the completion of the contract. Their value thus largely depends upon the standard of work executed by the contractor and his work may suffer if financial stringency arose during the course of the contract. In other words, retention moneys are vulnerable and cannot be regarded in the same class as normal trade debtors from the break-up standpoint.

The extent and quality of some debtors may also vary according to seasons. For example, an agricultural merchant supplying provender and implements to farmers may often have to grant extended credit, waiting until after the harvest to collect the moneys due from his farmer debtors. The liquidity of the debtors of such a business will, therefore, vary according to the harvest. Again, a bad summer may affect the quality of the trade debtors of a customer whose business largely comprises the supply of foodstuffs to seaside hotels and boarding houses. Any trading depression will increase the problems of the speedy collection of debtors.

Occasionally, the banker may find the item "bills receivable" included with trade debtors or shown separately in the balance sheet of a customer. The real value of this asset will depend equally upon the ability of the drawee (the trade debtor) to meet his bill at maturity, and the banker's assessment from the gone concern standpoint will be subject to all the tests already outlined with trade debtors. Bills receivable have one possible advantage in that their conversion into cash can be expedited by the discount of the bills, but the cost of such collection will again depend upon the quality of the names on the bills.

CASH AT BANK AND IN HAND

This last current asset is self-explanatory and the reader may be excused in jumping to the conclusion that no one can disturb the face value of cash. But surely in the event of failure of the customer any cash previously available will have been used to meet urgent outgoings and, apart from perhaps a few odd pence in the petty cash drawer, the liquidator or trustee will find the business devoid of cash. From the gone concern standpoint, therefore, it is necessary to estimate how any cash will be employed before the crash occurs. A relatively small cash balance may, of course, be ignored, but a worthwhile figure will be used either to meet a liability or to buy an asset. From discussions with the customer the banker may have a general idea of how the bulk of the money will be spent. It may be used to pay a dividend, or to discharge a tax liability, or to reduce creditors, or to buy fixed or current assets. The worth of the cash depends upon how it is used. If it is all applied to pay tax, then it must be worth its full face value because it will wipe out a preferential creditor for the same amount. It can, therefore, be added into the break-up total of assets without deduction. On the other hand, if it buys a machine or stock, it will be worth only the estimated forced sale value of the machine or stock, and such value only will be included in the break-up total of the assets. The banker has to decide according to the facts at his disposal and, as the cash balance will rarely be large in those cases where details of intended outlay are not available, the margin of possible error is small.

For example, in the case of XYZ Ltd. the view may be taken that the cash balance if £1,000 will shortly be used to pay the dividend of £800. It can, therefore, be valued at £800 and the balance of £200 ignored.

Additional Assets Acquired or Liabilities Paid from Increased Bank Borrowing
The same principles apply to the expenditure of any agreed bank facility which has not been fully utilised at the balance sheet date. In assessing the risk from the gone concern viewpoint, it must first be assumed that upon failure the customer will have borrowed the maximum amount permitted by the bank. In fact, in the absence of proper control, the customer may have taken a little more than the agreed maximum, but this possibility has to be ignored. It follows that any difference between the bank overdraft figure in the balance sheet and the agreed maximum that can be borrowed will have been used to acquire assets and/or to pay liabilities. The manner in which this increased bank borrowing is likely to be employed should be known to the banker from the negotiations conducted when the overdraft is arranged. The value of any additional bank borrowing on the assets side can be estimated accordingly. If it is used to buy stocks or fixed assets, their forced sale value can be assessed and, whilst the liabilities will be increased by the actual amount of the increase in the bank debt, the assets will be increased only by the estimated forced sale value of the assets so acquired. These principles can be illustrated by reference to XYZ Ltd. Suppose the maximum overdraft available to this company is £20,000, and the banker knows that the directors intend shortly to purchase new machinery costing £4,000 and will need the remaining £2,000 to clothe and run the additional machinery. The bank overdraft will be increased by £6,000 to £20,000 but the assets will be increased only by the bank's estimate of the forced sale value of the new machinery, which may be perhaps half its cost price, and by the estimated forced sale value of the stock in which the company deals. On the other hand, if XYZ Ltd. had no particular plans for expansion or the purchase of definite assets, the bank might assume that the additional bank advance would be used for normal trading, thereby increasing the book value of stock and work-in-progress by £6,000, or it might decide quite arbitrarily that £4,200 would be used to pay taxation, thereby creating an asset worth £4,200 to set-off against the tax liability shown in the balance sheet. The precise calculation will depend upon the view taken by the bank in the light of information available.

FICTITIOUS ASSETS
To complete the survey of typical assets, mention must be made of certain fictitious items which occasionally appear on the assets side of a balance sheet although they have no real value. It will be recalled that a balance sheet was defined at the outset as a classified summary of the balances

remaining in the ledgers of a business unit after all expenses and revenue have been transferred to trading and profit and loss account. A balance sheet is not merely a schedule of assets and liabilities, and certain debit balances may remain outstanding in the ledgers after the completion of the final accounts which have to be brought into the balance sheet as assets. They can naturally be ignored by the bank lender, but it is helpful to be able to appreciate their significance.

Preliminary Expenses
The cost of forming a limited company is in effect capital outlay and the law does not require that such expenditure should be written-off against revenue. From a theoretical point of view it is deemed to be an asset because the company could not have come into existence without meeting these preliminary costs. Usually it is written-off in the first few years of operation, but, until it is wiped out, the balance outstanding must be disclosed as a separate item in the balance sheet. (Part I.3 (a) of the Eighth Schedule of the Companies Act, 1948). A bank lender should query any failure on the part of a company customer to reduce the balance of this account.

Any expenses incurred in connection with an issue of share capital or debentures or amounts paid by way of commission in respect of shares or debentures have also to be shown separately in the balance sheet until they are written-off. The appearance of such items immediately causes the banker to wonder why such costs have not been charged against profits.

Profit and Loss Account
This fictitious asset is at once a danger sign to the lending banker, representing as it does accumulated loss carried forward. In effect it should be deducted from the capital of the business. Theoretically, the balance represents a debt to the business by the proprietors, but the shareholders in a limited company cannot be held responsible unless there is an uncalled liability on their shares, and the debit balance must remain as clear evidence of past losses until it can be wiped out by subsequent profits. In the case of a sole trader or partnership the financial resources of the proprietors outside the business may be sufficient to cover the deficit and fresh capital may be introduced to wipe out past losses. The reasons for the losses will be examined by the banker before granting accommodation; and from the going concern standpoint the capital resources of the borrower have to be reduced by the debit balance on profit and loss account.

This concludes the survey of the assets which are usually found in a balance sheet. The likely amount of cash to be produced upon a forced sale in the worst possible conditions has been estimated according to the facts available and, by totalling the amount thrown out against each asset, the banker at this stage knows about how much cash should be available to meet the creditors. In short, the imaginary auction is now over. The fictitious liquidator or trustee has completed the onerous work of realisation and, in place of the assets, has a cash balance at the bank. How is this cash to be distributed and what share will accrue to the bank? These questions cannot be answered until the liabilities have been analysed, which task demands a fresh chapter.

The Gone Concern Approach (part 3)

THE LIABILITES ANALYSED

The rights of creditors may vary considerably and it by no means follows that the bank will be entitled to share *pari passu* with all the other creditors in the estimated cash balance which has been realised from the theoretical forced sale of all the assets. There may be creditors who are secured by a charge on certain properties of the customer, others may hold a floating charge to secure what they have lent to a limited company. Some creditors may be entitled to certain legal priorities upon failure, whilst others may be exceedingly wise and, recognising the position, obtain payment in full by excessive pressure just before liquidation or bankruptcy. Each type of creditor must, therefore, be considered, and due allowance made for their rights. Whereas the assets from the gone concern standpoint are drastically depreciated, the liabilities ranking for payment must at least be taken at their face value. If the usual classes of liabilities which appear in a balance sheet are first analysed, the calculations necessary to enable the banker to estimate the risk attaching to the advance can be explained afterwards.

CAPITAL

The importance of this term, representing all that has been subscribed by the proprietors, plus profits retained for use in the business, has already been explained from the going concern standpoint. As the proprietors in the event of failure cannot obtain any dividend unless and until all creditors, including the bank, have received payment in full, the interests of the proprietors can virtually be ignored from the break-up stand point. Sometimes, however, the object of this gone approach is to assess the value of the shares in a private limited company, in which event the rights attaching to various types of shares have to be considered.

A complete picture of the capital position must be disclosed in the balance sheet of every limited company. Part I of the Eighth Schedule of the Companies Act, 1948, demands that the authorised capital and issued share capital be summarised separately, specifying any part of the issued capital that consists of redeemable preference shares and the earliest date upon which the company has power to redeem those shares. The amount of any share premium account must also be shown as a separate item. The nominal or authorised capital is the amount which the company has power to issue as shown in the Memorandum of Association and in some cases only a part thereof may have been subscribed or issued. The extent of the issued capital may be important to the lending banker where the borrowing powers of the directors are limited by the Articles to a proportion of or the total of such capital. The total will be clear from the balance sheet, from which all borrowing at the given date from any source can also be calculated.

Preference shares usually confer upon their holders a preferential right to receive repayment of the capital, sometimes with interest, before the ordinary or deferred shareholders. If need be, the precise rights can be ascertained from the Memorandum and Articles of Association of the company and they must be borne in mind before valuing the ordinary shares. Most preference shares carry the right to a fixed dividend out of the profits before any dividend is paid to the ordinary shareholders, and some confer the additional right to participate in any surplus profits after the payment of a certain rate to the other shareholders. The dividend is only claimable from profits, but in the case of cumulative preference shares if in any year the company cannot pay the agreed dividend the deficiency must be met out of subsequent profits before any dividend is paid to the ordinary shareholders. The articles may even provide that, in the event of winding-up, preference shareholders who have not received past dividends have the right to be paid all arrears of the preferential dividend, despite the fact that no profits were made, in priority to ordinary shareholders and in addition to their prior right to repayment of capital. These features, however, only concern the banker attempting to place a value on the shares of a company when it is estimated that there are surplus assets remaining after payment in full of all the company's debts.

A limited company cannot reduce its issued capital unless and until such power is contained in the Articles and the reduction is approved by special resolution of the members and confirmed by the Court. The usual causes leading to a reduction are either that the capital available is much in excess of needs for the purpose of the business or a substantial portion of the capital has been irretrievably lost. Any return of capital to shareholders or a diminution of their liability *prima facie* prejudices the interests of creditors of the company because it reduces the funds otherwise available to meet the debts of the company. Accordingly, every creditor has the right to object to any suggested reduction and the Court settles a list of creditors so entitled to object. Assuming that adequate funds are available, any dissentient creditor can always be satisfied by immediate payment. To avoid settling the creditors, a sound company with surplus capital may obtain a guarantee from its bankers to the Court to cover due payment of all creditors outstanding at the date of reduction of the capital. Where accumulated losses occasion the reduction, however, capital will be cancelled or written off (e.g. £1 fully paid shares reduced to fully paid shares of 50p each) and, as such a reduction results from capital already lost, the position of the creditors is not affected and, *prima facie*, they are not entitled to raise objection. The Court will not, of course, confirm any reduction which operates unfairly or irregularly against any particular class of shareholders, and it may require the company for a specified period to add the words "and reduced" after its name. A reduction of capital, however, is a problem which rarely confronts the practical banker

Where the capital of a company customer consists of partly paid shares, the amount remaining uncalled represents a reserve which will be available in case of need. Sometimes it may be a reserve liability where the company has resolved by special resolution that its uncalled capital can be called up only in the event of winding-up. Reserve capital cannot be attached by any charge created by the company. The amount of any uncalled capital will be clearly set out in the balance sheet, but its potential value depends entirely on the ability of the shareholders to meet their obligations when called upon. In the case of a small company, where the shareholders rarely change, a search at Companies House will reveal the names of the shareholders and the financial standing of those holding a large number of shares can be verified if necessary through the usual channels. The appearance of "Calls Unpaid" or "Forfeited Shares Account" items in a balance sheet is an indication that some shareholders have failed to meet their obligations. All these features are unusual these days and uncalled or reserved capital is rarely seen.

Many limited companies have power in their articles to issue redeemable preference shares, full details of any issue being disclosed in the balance sheet. Such shares cannot be redeemed unless fully paid and, as redemption would otherwise amount to a reduction of capital, they cannot be redeemed except out of profits otherwise available for dividend or out of the proceeds of a fresh issue of shares made to finance the redemption. Where such shares are redeemed otherwise than out of the proceeds of a fresh issue, a sum equal to the amount applied in redemption must be taken out of the profits otherwise available for dividend and transferred to a *"capital redemption reserve fund"* which is subject to the statutory restrictions as to any reduction of capital. In other words, upon redemption there is no net reduction in the capital employed in the company. Where any shares are redeemed out of the proceeds of a fresh issue, any premium payable on redemption must be provided out of profits earned before the redemption. These rules are all set out fully in Section 58 of the Companies Act, 1948, and this brief mention here serves to explain the significance of a capital redemption reserve fund in the balance sheet of a limited company customer.

In the case of a partnership or private trader, the capital will usually be shown in the balance sheet at the end of the other liabilities. There are, of course, no legal restrictions on any increase or decrease in their capital, although the prudent banker will naturally soon query excessive drawings by the proprietors. One of the fundamental disadvantages of a firm is that upon the death of a partner his personal representative may withdraw his capital, leaving the partnership with insufficient resources to continue trading. If the capital of the deceased is left in the business for the benefit of the new firm, it then represents a loan to the partnership and must be included in the liabilities for break-up purposes, thereby considerably weakening the position from the standpoint of the bank lender and the other unsecured creditors.

RESERVES AND PROVISIONS

There are various types of reserves and, although they all rank after the creditors from the gone concern aspect, it is advisable here to distinguish between the main kinds to assist the less experienced reader to interpret a balance sheet. The reserve most frequently seen is a revenue reserve comprising accumulated profits transferred usually in round amounts from the balance of profit and loss account. In effect, but not in name, any balance of undivided profits remaining in profit and loss account is a revenue reserve, and a deficiency in profit and loss account can always be corrected by transfers from revenue reserves. On the other hand, capital reserves, as their name implies, usually arise from capital transactions and are not generally regarded as available for transfer to profit and loss account to bolster poor trading results. Premiums collected on shares or debentures issued are inviolate capital reserves, and nowadays in view of the inflation of past decades it is not unusual for a company to revalue its fixed assets, applying any increase on their previous book value to capital reserve account. In similar manner, the disposal of fixed assets at a price exceeding their book value gives rise to a capital profit, usually transferred to a capital reserve. Thirdly, it is possible to distinguish a "reserve fund" as a term applied more correctly to a reserve which is represented by certain assets, preferably readily realisable, disclosed separately in the assets. In other words, funds are set aside out of profits for a particular purpose and held in cash or invested outside the business until that purpose is achieved. A factory may be built or a sports ground bought for the employees, etc., whereupon the funds on the asset side of the balance sheet are converted into the newly acquired fixed asset and the balance of the reserve fund can be transferred to other reserves, its purpose being achieved. Accumulated revenue and capital reserves may, of course, be capitalised by the issue of bonus shares to the members of the company. This is a popular course adopted nowadays to bring the issued capital of a company more into line with the value of its assets.

A provision is strictly speaking a reserve made for a specific purpose which may be to cover an actual or contingent future liability or to provide against the depreciation of certain assets. Any reserve or provision for taxation or dividend payments is an actual liability to be grouped with the other current liabilities of the business (see later). Provisions made for the depreciation of fixed assets or for diminution in the value of current assets (provision for bad or doubtful debts or stock reserve, etc.), may occasionally appear amongst the liabilities listed in the balance sheet, but they should be deducted from the value of the relative assets before the banker attempts to assess their forced sale value.

Apart from the special provisions referred to above, the total of capital and reserves employed in the business may be ignored from the break-up point of view. For example, in the balance sheet of XYZ Ltd., no part of the issued capital £17,000 and the General Reserve £7,500, plus £3,500 remaining on Profit and Loss Account—a total of £28,000—can be paid to the shareholders in the event of liquidation until all the creditors have received their 100p in the £.

LOAN CAPITAL

The analysis of all loan capital and the nature of any security created in favour of the lenders next demand close consideration. From the going concern viewpoint, loan capital can conveniently be included with capital and reserves to provide together the capital resources of the business, but all loans, whether of long or short term, secured or unsecured, have to be considered separately from the gone concern angle. The balance sheet of a limited company will at least reveal a clear initial picture because, as previously stated, where any debt is secured otherwise than by the operation of law a general note of the security must be made against the liability in the balance sheet. The more usual types of loan capital can now be examined.

Unsecured loans from directors or friends frequently appear in the balance sheets of private limited companies. Funds are thus lent to increase the resources of the business without troubling to increase the issued capital, but the terms of repayment are of vital importance. If repayable upon demand or at short term, they are current liabilities to be classified in effect with the bank debt and trade creditors, but it may not suit the bank as a lender to leave them in this category, and it may be prudent to ensure that they will remain undisturbed at least until the bank debt is repaid. To this end, the directors or other outside lenders may contract personally with the bank not to demand repayment and the company may likewise engage not to repay any such moneys without the prior consent of the bank. The claims of such loan creditors may also be postponed completely to the bank by their undertaking not to claim in the event of liquidation until the bank debt has been repaid in full. In such event, the loan creditors are deferred creditors akin to shareholders from the break-up standpoint, and the amounts due to them can be ignored in estimating the dividend payable in liquidation or bankruptcy. Alternatively, these loan creditors may undertake to the bank that in the event of liquidation they will prove *pari passu* with all other unsecured creditors but pay over to the bank the amount of any dividend they receive. In this way collateral security is obtained, often supported or consolidated by the joint and several guarantee of the loan creditors to cover accommodation granted to the company. It must be emphasised that these measures depend entirely upon the integrity of the loan creditors to implement their undertakings to the bank. By far the safest course is to insist that wherever possible the loan moneys are capitalised. Sometimes the borrowing concern may issue a promissory note to the loan creditor for the amount of the debt. It should be drawn repayable one day after demand and can then be deposited by the creditor with the bank as collateral security for advances to the promissor thereof. In the case of a sole trader or partnership borrower, certain unsecured loan creditors may in any event be deferred creditors whose rights are postponed to those of all the other unsecured creditors in the event of bankruptcy. These deferred creditors are defined by statute and include a wife who has advanced money to her husband for use in his trade or business, and *vice versa:* a partner who has lent money to his firm; and any person who has lent money to a firm in return for a rate of interest varying with the profits. Where satisfied that any given creditor would be deferred in event of failure his or her claims may be ignored when estimating the dividend likely to be payable to the other unsecured creditors.

Next can be considered the rights of any loan creditor secured by a specific charge on a certain asset or assets of the bank customer. For example, there may be a building society or private mortgage on the property. If the warning of such security quoted in the balance sheet does not give sufficient detail, the position in the case of a limited company can soon be ascertained by a search at the Companies Registry. Thereafter, it is a simple calculation to relate the estimated forced sale value of the security to the mortgage debt. If the amount owing exceeds the banker's estimate of the security proceeds, they will all be paid direct to the mortgagee and he will rank *pari passu* with the bank and other unsecured creditors for the balance remaining unpaid. On the other hand, if the estimated value of the security exceeds the loan, the mortgagee will be satisfied, leaving the surplus in the fund for the benefit of the other creditors. In other words, the amount of the secured loan or the value of the security, whichever is the smaller, can be set-off by deduction from the total break-up value of the assets and the total liabilities ranking for payment in liquidation. Apart from this gone concern assessment, the terms of repayment of any mortgage loan should, of course, be considered in relation to the current resources and earning capacity of the business. Unduly onerous terms for annual reductions may handicap the business and divert funds which are fully employed as working capital in the reduction of a long-term liability.

Lastly the rights of the debenture holder in the limited company balance sheet call for special consideration. Legally, a debenture is any document which contains an acknowledgment of indebtedness by a company and it may be unsecured or naked, containing a mere promise to pay, or secured by a mortgage or charge on some or all of the company's assets. In the most unusual event that the debenture holders are unsecured, the amount due to them is taken at face value, ranking with all other unsecured creditors for payment. Normally, debentures are secured by a fixed charge upon the land and premises of the borrowing company and a floating charge upon all the remaining assets present and future, sometimes including any uncalled capital. The property may be charged by way of legal mortgage to trustees for the debenture holders and the conditions endorsed on each debenture refer to the trust deed. The trustees safeguard the interests of the debenture holders, hold the title deeds, and are usually empowered when the need arises to realise the security or appoint a receiver. An initial warning of the nature of the security given to the debenture holders will appear in the balance sheet but full details can easily be obtained from the files at the Companies Registry.

Again, the gone concern calculation depends upon the relationship between the amount of the debentures outstanding and the banker's estimate of the forced sale value of the security. If specific assets only are charged, then by a process of cancellation such specific assets must be wiped-off the break-up total at their estimated forced sale value. If the amount of the debentures exceeds the value placed upon the given assets, such excess must be included with the other unsecured creditors. But where the break-up value exceeds the total due to the debenture holders, such excess may remain in the total of assets. It is merely a direct set-off of whichever is the smaller amount, leaving any excess available in the assets or ranking with the unsecured creditors, as the case may be. Where the debentures are secured by a fixed and floating charge on the assets, however, their full total will be deducted from both the liabilities and the total estimated forced sale value of the assets, assuming sufficient is left after settlement of all other secured and preferential creditors. The incidence of these latter complications will be explained fully later when valuing a mortgage and charge held by a bank as security, but it is clear that where there is a relatively heavy debenture issue before the bank, advances will not usually be granted to the company unless other approved security of adequate worth is available to the bank.

Particular care is required where a balance sheet discloses that debentures have been redeemed and are capable of being reissued (*see* XYZ Ltd. balance sheet). Debentures may be redeemable or irredeemable and in the former case are redeemed according to the terms of issue—by periodical drawings or by repayment on either the fixed date or subject to the necessary notice being given to the debenture holders at the option of the company. The danger is that a company has power to reissue debentures which have been redeemed either by reissuing the same debentures, or by issuing others in their place, unless the Articles, or the terms on which the debentures were issued, or any other contract entered into by the company, forbid such reissue. *Any debenture which is reissued conveys the same priorities as those possessed by the original holder.* In other words reissued debentures rank *pari passu* with the original issue. Where a company has power to reissue debentures which have been redeemed, particulars of the debentures available for reissue must be shown in every balance sheet of the company, and the lending banker should look out for such details. Any debentures reissued after the banker has granted the advance will rank before the bank for repayment because the new holders have the same rights and priorities as the original holders. Apart from any question of break-up, the balance sheet must always be examined for redeemed debentures which are capable of reissue, so that if some are disclosed, arrangements can be made to have them cancelled or reissued to the bank and the power to reissue any outstanding debentures removed by resolution of the company. In this way the banker ensures that the maximum amount ranking prior to his claim is limited to the total debentures or other secured loans outstanding at the time of the advance.

And so ends this survey of the rights of the loan creditors.

THE CURRENT LIABILITIES

The current liabilities of the borrower now have to be examined from the gone concern aspect and from the general standpoint of the lending banker. They include all debts at short-term arising in the normal course of business outside the generic term "fixed capital". Some may have preferential rights and some may have security whilst others may be paid long before the crash occurs. They will normally include the following items:—

Taxation

In this age of heavy taxation the liabilities of every profitable business will include provision for taxation of some kind. The demands of this uninvited, unwelcome partner who plays little part in the development of the business but nevertheless expects to receive a major share of any profit, call for special consideration. Many problems arise with different types of borrowers.

Firstly, it must not be forgotten that the Inland Revenue are preferential creditors entitled to payment in full before any other creditors, other than those secured by fixed charges. Section 319 of the Companies Act, 1948 provides that in the winding-up of a limited company there shall be paid in priority to all other debts, *inter alia*, corporation tax or other taxes, assessed on the company up to the 5th day of April next before the winding-up date, and *not exceeding in the whole one year's assessment*, and the amount of any value added tax due from the company at the relevant date. Precisely the same rights accrue to the Inland Revenue in the event of a bankruptcy. In general, therefore, one year's tax is preferential and the total may include, in addition to the items specified above, amounts collected from employee's wages under P.A.Y.E. or national insurance schemes but not paid over to the appropriate authorities. In particular, it may be emphasised here that this preferential claim for all taxes must be settled before a bank or any other lender can obtain anything from the proceeds of a floating charge on the company's assets. Obviously, therefore, the likely preferential liability of the borrowing company must be assessed with care and duly allowed for when estimating the bank's position.

Some may argue that, if a customer experiences lean trading and the position deteriorates over a few years, the tax liability will be offset by losses and little, if anything, will be due to the Inland Revenue upon failure. But this theory rarely obtains in practice because, particularly where overtrading is the cause of bankruptcy or liquidation, cash due to the tax inspector has been used to meet pressing creditors or to finance undue expansion, and a relatively heavy tax liability still remains outstanding. In fact, when a receiver is appointed by the bank, the whole of the proceeds realised from a floating charge may be swallowed up by this preferential creditor. Income tax, surtax (in the case of sole proprietors and firms) and corporation tax are all payable long after the actual profit is earned and there is an appreciable delay in the collection of VAT and P.A.Y.E. deductions. In the meantime the cash is normally employed in the business and may be lost or converted into fixed, unsaleable assets when the liability is determined and due for payment. In practice, adequate provision for estimated tax will usually be made in the profit and loss appropriation account at the end of the trading year, but this does not mean that cash is set aside in a separate banking account to meet the debt when it actually falls due. Corporation tax assessed in respect of the company's trading year ended on 31st December, 1977, becomes due for payment on 1st January, 1979, being due on 1st January, each year in respect of the profits earned in the trading period ended twelve months previously. The balance sheet of the company at, say, 31st December, 1977, should include, therefore, the current liability for corporation tax due for payment on 1st January, 1978, in respect of the profits of the trading year 1976 and the deferred liability for corporation tax due for payment on 1st January, 1979, in respect of the profits of the trading year 1977. If the company has annual charges, for example, interest payable under deduction of income tax, it is liable to account for this tax to the Inland Revenue and may, therefore, have a further income tax liability at balance sheet date. Hence it is clear that unless cash is reserved in some way for tax when due for payment, the tax liability can accumulate and the amount unpaid may be large when failure occurs. Cash for tax may have been swallowed up in development outlay and sufficient quick assets cannot be realised in time to meet the liability. Granted, the Inland Revenue are preferential creditors for only one year's assessment, but they can choose the heaviest year unpaid in the previous six years and rank *pari passu* with the other creditors for the remainder which may be due to them.

The prudent banker will normally rely on the customer's auditors to ensure that adequate provision has been made for all tax due to the balance sheet date and can then regard the entire amount so provided as preferential from the gone concern standpoint. A well set out balance sheet will leave no doubt on the matter because tax actually due and payable will be included in current liabilities, although the estimated amount set aside to cover the liability to corporation tax on current profits may appear as a separate item, showing the due date for payment. However, it is not usually possible to analyse all the tax items to decide when they are actually payable, and the safest and simplest course is to treat all such provisions as preferential, paying them in full from the estimated cash proceeds of the mythical forced sale of the assets before the unsecured creditors are entitled to their share. Thus, in the case of XYZ Ltd. there will be £4,200 preferential tax to be paid in this manner.

Apart altogether from the method of dealing with the taxation liability from the gone concern angle, it is, of course, imperative that the banker should be satisfied, before granting any advance, that the customer realises the need to retain cash or readily realisable assets to meet the tax liability and will not expect the bank later to increase the accommodation in order to finance tax disbursements. So often where a business is developing rapidly, cash is swallowed up in fixed assets and liquid resources remaining are insufficient to cover tax payments. Although the Inland Revenue is usually a patient creditor, the amount due to it is often relatively large and cannot be allowed to accumulate unpaid over the years. This danger arises frequently with sole trader customers who withdraw for personal expenses the current profits in their business long before they receive their assessments for surtax. The prudent banker must be a wise counsellor and friend in this respect and the warning note can alway be sounded from an intelligent survey of such a customer's trading and profit and loss accounts and balance sheet.

When a company declares a dividend the amount payable to the shareholders is debited to the profit and loss account and, in due course, is remitted to the shareholders. This payment triggers a liability for Advanced Corporation Tax (ACT) which is to be remitted to the Inland Revenue at the end of the quarter after the dividend has been paid. ACT can be set against the corporation tax liability on income. The balance sheet item "ACT Recoverable" will only arise where the dividend which has been charged to the profit and loss appropriation account is paid in the company's ensuing financial year or the ACT exceeds the amount of corporation tax available for set-off. If the offset of ACT is reasonably certain within the next accounting period it should be counted as a deferred asset in the company's accounts.

This is hardly the place to dilate upon the effects of excessive taxation but it is well to remember that VAT increases the amount required as working capital to carry stocks, whilst corporation tax often removes from the business moneys which are needed to finance the replacement of assets to cover the costs of expansion.

It is of interest to note in passing that all local rates due upon winding-up or bankruptcy and having become due and payable within twelve months next before such date are likewise preferential, but usually they are relatively too small to trouble the banker in estimating the position. Unless special circumstances apply, the possible preferential claims of employees for unpaid wages or salary and for accrued holiday remuneration, can likewise be ignored in the banker's estimate. On the other hand, where a bank has made advances to a limited company specifically to pay wages within Section 319 (1) (b) of the Companies Act, 1948, the total of such advances can be included as preferential for the bank in the break-up calculation.

Hire Purchase Creditors

This item frequently appears in balance sheets where customers, with limited capital resources resort to hire purchase facilities for the acquisition of new plant and machinery, motors or lorries. The item must naturally first be considered in relation to the resources and earning capacity of the business. Excessive resort to the expedient is a danger sign. Instead of obtaining fixed capital to finance fixed assets a current liability is created, reducing working capital and perhaps sowing the seeds of over-trading. Difficulty may be experienced in financing the monthly instalments to the detriment of the bank's position. From the gone concern angle, the hire purchase creditors are secured according to the terms of the agreement on certain assets and have to be paid out of those assets. In fact they can usually seize the assets which are the subject of an H.P. contract with unpaid instalments. Details will not usually be available to the banker, but it will be prudent to accept the worst view and assume that the whole of the estimated forced sale value of the plant, machinery and the motors or sufficient thereof (whichever is the smaller figure) is taken out of the common pool to meet the hire purchase creditors. For example, in the case of XYZ Ltd., if it was estimated that the plant and machinery and motors would realise at auction only £1,500, then the whole of this amount would be applied in reduction of the hire purchase creditors £2,000, leaving the balance of £500 to rank *pari passu* for dividend with the other unsecured creditors. On the other hand, if the forced sale value of the relative assets was estimated at say £3,000, the hire purchase creditors would be fully paid, leaving £1,000 in the pool for the bank and other unsecured creditors. It cannot always be assumed that a hire purchase creditor will be fully secured in the event of failure. The market for his security may be flooded and the plant, etc., worth only scrap value. Admittedly, this creditor may not be entitled to claim for anything other than possession of the assets subject to the agreement, but the banker can hardly analyse all the terms thereof before making the estimate. The strict legal position may differ from the view taken by the bank but the difference will not materially affect the bank's estimate. Any assets subject to a hire purchase agreement must, of course, be excluded from the valuation of a floating charge in favour of the bank.

Trade Creditors
This will usually be the largest current liability appearing in the balance sheet of a trading customer representing the total owing to those who have supplied goods and services to the business. The need to relate the total outstanding to the total of goods purchased during the trading period has already been explained under the going concern review. The dangers of unduly large creditors on long-term credit are obvious and the need to be satisfied that the amounts are well spread may be important. Where large amounts are owing to a few creditors, the sudden demand by those creditors for full payment may result in financial strain leading to failure. Unhappy, pressing creditors are an obvious sign of weakness.

Apart from these general features which are within the ambit of the going concern approach, there remains the likely effect which deterioration in the financial strength of the customer may have in the trade concerned. Bad news travels very fast in trade circles and it may soon get round that the borrower is experiencing difficulty in meeting his accounts. Delays in payment may be whispered from creditor to creditor, between their travellers or representatives, with the net result that the wiser creditor brings pressure to bear for payment. To withstand the immediate onslaught and satisfy the major demands, the failing customer perhaps sells stock at a loss or presses the collection of certain debtors or in some way gets out of the assets sufficient cash to pay those wise creditors in full. This process obviously cannot go on for long, but whilst it lasts certain creditors get 100p in the £ and the forced sale value of the assets is correspondingly reduced before the liquidation or bankruptcy. This tendency, proved from experience, may be taken into account by the banker deciding quite arbitrarily and probably excessively, by erring on the safe side, that a given proportion of the creditors shown in the balance sheet will be paid in full in this manner. There is no golden rule. It is a matter of policy, but the larger the secured creditors of a limited company, with warning registrations at the Companies Registry, perhaps the larger might be the estimate of creditors so paid. After making the estimate, the remainder of the operation is merely an arithmetical calculation. The creditors are reduced by the agreed amount, which is likewise deducted from the imaginary cash pool representing the estimated forced sale value of the assets. Some lenders may, of course, prefer to ignore this allowance leaving the entire amount of trade creditors to rank at face value for dividend with the bank.

Dividend Payable

This self-explanatory item is usually relatively small and can quickly be disposed of in the banker's estimate. To pay the dividend, cash or the equivalent will soon be removed from the assets. Unquestionably the dividend will be paid long before the risk of failure ever arises. Nevertheless, to preserve basic principles it is again a question of set-off, deducting the amount of the dividend from both sides of the balance sheet. In the case of XYZ Ltd., it may be assumed that the cash in hand £1,000 is used for simplicity to pay the dividend of £800, and both items, therefore, in effect disappear from the picture. The theory need not be pursued further.

Bank Debt

The last current liability for consideration is the bank debt, actual and potential, details of which are fully known to the lending banker. If there is any margin between the figure shown in the balance sheet and the maximum which the customer may overdraw, the difference has to be added to make the bank debt up to the agreed limit. It may reasonably be assumed that if and when the customer fails, the bank overdraft will be at, if not beyond, the arrangement. Any bank money to be spent after the balance sheet date will, of course, produce certain assets or reduce liabilities. The bank will know from negotiations with the customer approximately how the additional withdrawals are to be spent. They may be used wholly or partly to pay taxation or to buy further fixed assets, or to finance normal trading, usually thereby increasing stock. The forced sale value of the assets will be increased by the estimated proceeds according to how the money is expected to be used. These principles were explained more fully in the previous chapter.

    This completes the review of the current liabilities normally found in the balance sheet of the average customer. It may be, however, that there are contingent liabilities to be taken into consideration, paticularly in the case of a limited company balance sheet.

CONTINGENT LIABILITIES

Section 149 of the Companies Act 1948 and the Eighth Schedule, paragraph 11 thereto, require that there shall be stated in a company balance sheet by way of note, *inter alia*, particulars of any charge on the assets of the company to secure the liabilities of any other person, including where practicable the amount secured, and the general nature of any other contingent liabilities not provided for and the aggregate amount or estimated amount of those liabilities, if it is material. Furthermore, a note is required, if possible, of the aggregate amount or estimated amount, where material of contracts authorised by the directors for capital expenditure, so far as not provided for.

In other words, it is incumbent upon the lending banker to read closely all notes which appear in the balance sheet and, if they refer to contingent liabilities, to apply the information to the break-up estimate. There may be guarantee liabilities outstanding or contingent liabilities on other engagements and it may, therefore, be prudent to increase the total liabilities by an amount equivalent to the estimated liability likely to be determined on the worst basis. Much naturally depends upon the nature of the contingent liability and the bank's knowledge of the position. If there are outstanding commitments for capital expenditure, it may be that they will be defrayed from the additional bank borrowing available. In the absence of any margin in the bank advance, perhaps the capital outlay will be covered by realisations of stocks and debtors. In any event, the settlement of such commitments will presumably produce some asset of proportionate estimated value. It is all a question of facts so far as they may be known to or ascertained by the banker. The same principles apply throughout. It is prudent to add to the liabilities every possible debt, actual or contingent, but to increase the forced sale value of the assets by the minimum amount only which is likely to be realised from such actual or contingent expenditure. The worst possible position obviously provides the safest estimate of the bank's risk, and the test is whether such risk can be accepted having regard to all the many attendant circumstances.

The Gone Concern Approach (part 4)

CONCLUSIONS DRAWN FROM THE FOREGOING ANALYSIS

The detailed analysis of all the balance sheet items has now been completed and, in order to assess the bank's risk in the event of the failure of the borrower after the advance has been granted, it is necessary to estimate the dividend likely to be payable to unsecured creditors. This is merely a question of mathematics. On the asset side there is a total of cash representing the estimated proceeds of the forced sale of the assets and, on the other side, there are the creditors, some of whom may hold security on certain assets or enjoy preferential rights. All the principles outlined in these pages can now be applied to the following example to show how the banker calculates the estimated dividend payable.

P Q R Limited

Balance Sheet as at 31st December, 1977

LIABILITIES (actual)	£	ASSETS (estimated by bank to produce on a forced sale basis)	£	£
Capital and Reserves, including balance on Profit and Loss Account	20,000	Goodwill		Nil
		Freehold Factory (mortgaged— see contra)		5,000
Debentures—secured by a floating charge on the assets of the company	10,000	Plant and Machinery		1,500
Loan Creditor secured by a legal mortgage on the factory	6,000	Motors (new)		4,000
Hire Purchase Crs. (all on motors)	3,000	Fixtures & Fittings		500
Taxation (all regarded as preferential)	4,500	Total estimated yield from fixed assets		11,000
Trade Creditors (equivalent to ten weeks' purchases—longer than normal trade credit)	16,500	Trade Debtors (well spread and good names)		16,000
Dividend Payable (since paid)	2,000	STOCK		
		Raw materials		4,000
Total	42,000	Finished goods		6,000
Add: proposed bank advance	10,000	Cash on hand (all used to pay dividend)		2,000
	52,000	Total estimated yield of balance sheet assets		39,000
		Add: yield from bank advance to be used—		
		To pay tax	4,500	4,500
		To pay creditors	2,500	2,500
		For stocks (which the bank values cautiously at one-third of cost price)	3,000	1,000
			10,000	47,000

P.Q.R. Ltd., manufacturers of ladies garments, approaches its bankers for overdraft accommodation up to £10,000 without security and, after confirming that the financial position of the company is reasonably sound from the going concern aspect, the bank analyses the latest balance sheet figures and draws up the estimate of the position, detailed above.

It will be seen that at this stage the estimated dividend for all creditors is 90p in the £, there being £47,000 cash available from the assets to meet creditors totalling £52,000. The dividend available for the unsecured creditors, including the bank, is, however, greatly reduced when the prior claims of the secured and preferential creditors have been satisfied. The final calculation is thus made:—

	£	£		£
Total creditors		52,000	Estimated total cash yield from all assets	47,000
	10,000		*Deduct:*	
	5,000		*1. Secured Creditors*	
			Debentures (secured on all assets) 10,000	
	3,000		Mortgage Creditor—value of security only	5,000
	4,500		Hire Purchase Creditors (fully covered)	3,000
			2. Preferential Creditors	
	2,000		Taxation	4,500
			3. Creditors paid before the failure	
	2,500		Dividend	2,000
		27,000	Trade Creditors (from bank advance)	2,500
				27,000
Creditors outstanding (including bank (£10,000))		25,000	Cash remaining	20,000

It follows that, as only £20,000 remains to meet unsecured creditors totalling £25,000, the estimated dividend payable is 80p in the £, and on this basis the bank's risk on a limit of £10,000 would be £2,000. Whether the bank is prepared to accept this estimated risk is entirely a matter of policy, and the position will be considered in conjunction with many other factors relating to the proposal. It may be thought prudent to obtain collateral security to cover the estimated risk, or the bank may be satisfied that the company will use the money to advantage and quickly repay the indebtedness from trading receipts. The point is that the bank as a prudent lender has estimated its risk in the worst possible event, and is thus able to reach a decision based on this assessment and on the other material factors which apply to the proposal. It by no means follows that the result of this final assessment completely governs the final attitude of the bank. The gone concern analysis is the only one of the many means available to assist the bank in reaching the correct decision. Advances may be declined notwithstanding the fact that the balance sheet of the potential borrower shows 100p in the £ on a break-up basis. On the other hand, many advances may be granted where the forced sale value of the assets is insufficient to pay the unsecured creditors in full. The first test is always made from the going concern standpoint and, if this is satisfactory, the estimated dividend is calculated as a secondary, but complementary, test to guide the bank. A few practical examples to emphasise the value of these tests and to illustrate many of the features which have been discussed in these pages, will be found in the next chapter.

VALUATION OF A FLOATING CHARGE

Where a bank is relying on a floating charge as security for accommodation granted to a limited company customer, the value of the charge can be estimated only from a gone concern analysis of the balance sheet of the borrower. The principles are precisely the same as those which apply to the calculation of the dividend payable to unsecured creditors. The bank has to look forward in an attempt to estimate from experience how much a receiver would collect if one was appointed to realise the assets caught by the floating charge. In such an event, the receiver would have to dispose of most of the assets by auction to unwilling buyers and the prices realised would be much less than the balance sheet value of the items. Out of the cash proceeds all costs and the preferential creditors would have to be met before the balance could be paid over to the bank. Moreover, the receiver would not be able to claim for the bank the proceeds of any assets which were subject to a fixed charge in favour of a third party. His interest would be limited to the equity, if any, available after complete satisfaction of the mortgagee. The following example shows how these principles can be applied:

Northtown Bank are asked to lend £10,000 to T.U.V. Ltd. to finance increased turnover arising from a heavy seasonal demand for their mowers. The only security available is a floating charge on the assets of the company and its latest balance sheet is analysed and tabulated by the bank as follows:

T U V Limited

Balance Sheet as at 31st January, 1978

LIABILITIES		ASSETS		*Notes made by bank*	*Bank estimate of forced sale value*
	£		£		£
Capital and Reserves	30,000	Goodwill	10,000		Nil
		Freehold Factory	12,000		
				Old building Cost £14,000 in 1948. Poor site for labour. Adaptable	6,000
Loan Creditor (secured by mortgage on factory)	4,000				
		Plant and Machinery	8,700	Depreciated 10 per cent. per annum. Highly specialised. Poor market for forced sale	2,000
Hire Purchase Creditors (new machinery)	1,600				
Taxation (all regarded as preferential)	6,000	Motors	1,500	5 Lorries heavily used	500
		Fixtures & Fittings	800	Ignore	—
Trade Creditors (equivalent to one month's purchases)	9,600	Total fixed assets	33,000	(Working capital only £1,000)	8,500
Bank Overdraft	500				
	21,700	Stock and Work-in-progress	8,400	All garden tools. Mostly mowers. Limited market	5,000
Add bank advance to be made to increase to required maximum of £10,000	9,500	Trade Debtors	10,300	Well spread amongst 150 names. Few bad debts in past	9,000
	31,200		51,700		22,500

Add estimated value of stock bought with bank advance £95,900 say 7,000

Total estimated cash on forced sale 29,500

From this estimated position the bank calculates the value of its floating charge by deducting from the total cash realised from the imaginary forced sale, the amounts which would have to be paid to the preferential and secured creditors who rank prior to the bank.

	£	£
Total cash proceeds of assets		29,500
Less: Loan Creditor (secured by a mortgage on the factory)	4,000	
Hire Purchase Creditors (on machinery—assumed to be fully covered)	1,600	
Taxation (entirely preferential)	6,000	
Estimated trade creditors paid out of realisation of assets before appointment of receiver by bank, say	1,000	
Receiver's costs and charges, say	2,900	
		15,500
Estimated value of floating charge		**14,000**

VALUATION OF SHARES IN PRIVATE LIMITED COMPANY

The same principles can be applied where a bank wishes to estimate the minimum value of unquoted shares held as security. In an imaginary liquidation, any surplus of the forced sale value of the assets of the company available after the payment of all creditors will be distributed amongst the shareholders according to their respective rights. For example, an analysis of the balance sheet of a private limited company with the following issued capital:

	£
10,000 5 per cent. Preference Shares of £1 each fully paid	10,000
25,000 Ordinary Shares of £1 each fully paid	25,000
	35,000

discloses that, in the opinion of the banker, the assets would realise £120,000 in the event of liquidation. The total creditors of the company are £100,000, so that there would be a surplus of £20,000 available for the shareholders. As the preference shareholders are entitled to prior rights, they will take the first £10,000, leaving £10,000 to be distributed between the ordinary shareholders. It follows that the preference shares are worth par, whilst the ordinary shares are worth only 40p each. This rough and ready estimate may be the only means available to assess the value of the bank's security.

These three simple examples suffice to illustrate the application of the basic principles to typical banking problems. As previously emphasised there can be no slide rule for general use with all balance sheets. Each balance sheet demands an independent survey and the attitude of the banker and the final result of the analysis will differ considerably according to the detailed facts of the case and the practical policy of the lender.

Chapter X   Balance Sheets

Some Practical Examples

To complete the survey of balance sheets from the standpoint of the lending banker, and to illustrate the basic principles which have been explained in these articles, it is helpful at this stage to draw upon the imaginary experiences of the fictitious Mr. Cashe, the manager of Northtown Bank, and to see how he dealt with the requirements of certain customers when they presented their balance sheets in support of their request for bank accommodation.

1. *The Undoubted Borrower.*
The directors of Perfectione K. F. & S. Ltd., an old established company customer manufacturing cutlery for the home and foreign markets, approach Northtown Bank for an overdraft limit of £50,000 to finance a substantial order for the supply of cafe equipment to a chain store in America. The peak figure will be required for a few weeks pending deliveries of the finished goods and the entire order will be completed and paid for within nine months. At the interview the directors produce the balance sheet (opposite) of their company and Mr. Cashe is duly impressed.

From a long experience, Mr. Cashe reads this balance sheet in a methodical manner. A glance at the issued capital and undistributed profits is sufficient to enable him to realise that the resources of his customers total no less than £½ million, and the absence of any other liabilities, apart from taxation and trade creditors, indicates that this capital has so far been ample to finance their trading. There are no secured creditors ranking before the bank and the clear presentation of the figures in modern manner enables him to decide without resort to pencil and paper that the working capital of the company is £360,000 (Capital Resources: £500,000, less fixed assets, including trade investments, £140,000). The position is so liquid that Mr. Cashe thirsts to lend to the company, but prudently he completes his survey. Preferential creditors are limited to taxation, at most £140,000, against which there are Treasury Bills valued at £120,000, plus cash on hand £40,000. Sales in the accompanying trading account total £1½ million for the year to the balance sheet date so that roughly stock-on-hand is equivalent to one month's turnover (no question of stockpiling here), but the debtor figure is equal to nearly three months' sales and Mr. Cashe tactfully enquires why this amount is relatively so large. The directors explain that an

Perfectione K. F. & S. Limited

Balance Sheet as at 30th November, 1977

LIABILITIES	£	ASSETS	£	£
CAPITAL AUTHORISED AND ISSUED				
100,000 6 per cent. Cum. Pref. shares		**FIXED ASSETS**		
of £1 each	100,000	Freehold Factory and Offices at		
250,000 Ordinary shares of £1 each,		cost	140,000	
fully paid	250,000	Less: cumulative depreciation		
		to date	40,000	
	350,000			100,000
General Reserve	100,000	Plant, Machinery, Furniture and		
Profit and Loss Account	50,000	Fittings, at cost	45,000	
		Less: cumulative depreciation		
Total of Capital Reserves and Surplus	500,000	to date	15,000	
Reserve for Future Income Tax, Esti-				30,000
mated Liability 1975-76	50,000	Motors at cost		2,000
		Total of Fixed Assets		132,000
		Trade Investments		8,000
		Net Current Assets—		
		Current Assets		
		Stocks and work-in-progress, as		
		certified by the Directors, at or		
		under cost	126,000	
		Sundry Debtors	360,000	
		Treasury Bills	120,000	
		Cash at Bank	40,000	
			646,000	
		Less Current Liabilities		
		Corporation Tax	90,000	
		Sundry Creditors	126,000	
		Proposed Ord. Divi-		
		dend less tax	20,000	
			236,000	
				410,000
	550,000			**550,000**

influenza epidemic in their office delayed the despatch of invoices in October so that their collection of debtors had fallen one month behind, whilst in November heavy export orders doubled their deliveries. All these collections are now up-to-date and the debtor figure has been reduced to almost £160,000, whilst work-in-progress and stock has increased to £300,000 in keeping with their larger order book. Failing to find any reference to bad or doubtful debts in either the profit and loss account or the balance sheet, Mr. Cashe next enquires quite casually whether the company make provision for doubtful accounts. He is promptly told that as the company sell only to undoubted home buyers and cover all export orders up to 90 per cent. with the Export Credits Guarantee Department, they have not found it necessary to build up any bad debt reserve. Nevertheless, in the course of conversation, Mr Cashe pursues the point by discreet reference to their types of buyers and from the ensuing discussion he is able to reach the general conclusion that one-third of their debtors are foreign, well spread around the globe, and the remaining two-thirds include around 400 well-known houses in this country. Addressing himself next to the trade creditors, Mr. Cashe introduces the problem of supplies of raw materials, whilst he compares the annual purchases figure with the amount due in the balance sheet to creditors. He quickly realises that with total purchases of £1¼ million the company is taking the usual monthly trade credit but is not surprised to hear that it is now buying steel up to three months in advance.

Unperturbed, this exemplary bank manager changes the conversation to the vagaries of the weather or the prospects for the Cup Final, whilst he mentally checks the position from the gone concern standpoint. He regroups the assets and liabilities in his mind. Current liabilities total £286,000, of which tax £140,000 plus dividend £20,000 are immediately paid out of Treasury Bills £120,000 and cash in hand £40,000. This merely leaves £126,000 trade creditors and the proposed peak bank debt of £50,000 to be met out of stock and debtors £486,000, increased proportionately by the expenditure of the bank advance. The fixed assets can be ignored and a healthy surplus is assured. Being completely satisfied on all points and safe in the knowledge that his directors will support him, Mr. Cashe makes his customers welcome to the accommodation without thought of security, and congratulates the directors on the inherent financial strength of the company.

2. *The Marginal Case.*

Later the same morning, Mr. Bull, the director and virtual owner of China Shops Ltd., a private company with a widespread chain of retail glass and china shops, calls at Northdown Bank seeking overdraft accommodation to finance the purchase of a competitive business comprising six retail shops in the suburbs of London owned by a Mr. Dish, As China Shops Ltd. have hitherto conducted a satisfactory, if somewhat slender, credit account, Mr. Cashe has no knowledge of their financial position and has literally never heard of the Dish business. He has, therefore, to start from scratch and, in response to his request, Mr. Bull produces the following balance sheets and the accompanying trading and profit and loss accounts.

China Shops Limited
Balance Sheet as at 31st December, 1977

LIABILITIES	£	ASSETS	£
AUTHORISED & ISSUED CAPITAL			
5,000 Shares at £1 each, fully paid	5,000	Shops, at cost *less* depreciation	10,000
		Fixtures & Fittings *less* depreciation	1,500
Mortgages	4,000	Motors, *less* depreciation	1,500
Hire Purchase Creditor	1,000	Stock	3,500
Trade Creditors	7,300	Trade Debtors	500
Taxation	200	Profit and Loss Account	500
	17,500		17,500

The Square Plate Company
(Sole Proprietor, Mr. R. A. Dish)

Balance Sheet as at 31st January, 1978

LIABILITIES	£	ASSETS	£
Trade Creditors	3,000	Goodwill	3,000
Capital	7,000	Shops, at cost	4,500
		Fixtures & Fittings	500
		Stock	1,500
		Cash on hand	500
	10,000		**10,000**

With sinking heart and a few unkind thoughts concerning the paucity of information disclosed in these balance sheets, Mr. Cashe enquires what China Shops Ltd. propose to purchase and how much of the price to be paid is required from Northtown Bank. It transpires that the customers have contracted to buy the entire net assets of Mr. Dish's business for £10,000, the price being calculated as follows:

	£
Goodwill	3,000
Two freehold lock-up shops at valuation	6,000
Four annual tenancies of shops	800
Fixtures & Fittings	500
Stocks at valuation, say	2,200
	12,500
Less: trade creditors	2,500
	10,000

The trading results of the business for the past four years suffice to convince the bank manager that the purchase price is reasonable and he readily recognises that the proposed extension of the China Shops Ltd. business will be beneficial to its proprietors, but he is nonplussed to hear that Mr. Bull expects the bank to find the entire amount required to complete the purchase. Politely but very firmly, Mr. Cashe thereupon delivers a financial homily which he later summarises as follows in his records:

With a net stake of £4,500 in their business (capital £5,000, less debit balance on profit and loss account £500), it was unreasonable of the directors of China Shops to expect the bank to find £10,000 to cover their proposed capital outlay. The company was already, alas, void of working capital because, with fixed assets valued at £13,000, the net fixed capital amounted only to £8,500, a deficiency of £4,500 patently made up by hire purchase creditors, £1,000 and unduly long trade credit. It would appear that with trade creditors £7,300, equivalent to three months' credit, they were buying on the longest possible terms and it may be that already creditors were growing restive. The existing lack of capital and the resulting precarious financial position was obvious. To contemplate further relatively heavy outlay without the introduction of adequate fresh capital would be the height of folly, and the bank certainly would not assist in the financial suicide of its customer. As Mr. Bull found it a little difficult to follow this argument, the bank manager made a rough note of the position of China Shops Ltd. after completion of the Dish purchase.

LIABILITIES	£	ASSETS	£
Net capital	4,500	Goodwill	3,000
Mortgages	4,000	Shops	16,800
		Fixtures & Fittings	2,000
Total Fixed Capital	8,500	Motors	1,500
Hire Purchase Creditors	1,000		
Trade Creditors	9,800	*Total Fixed Assets*	23,300
Taxation	200	Stock	5,700
Bank Advance	10,000	Trade Debtors	500
	29,500		**29,500**

How could a business with a fixed capital of £8,500 hope to carry fixed assets £23,300? The bank advance would at all times be repayable on demand, whilst trade creditors would inevitably be restive. Gradually Mr. Bull appreciated the soundness of these criticisms and readily co-operated in an attempt to solve the problem and, by dint of perserverance, Mr. Cashe eventually moulded a sound banking proposal which he felt justified in recommending to his directors. To avoid wearying the reader with a detailed account of the interview, the following outline suffices to record what transpired:

1. It was acknowledged that: £
   (a) to correct the present capital deficiency of China Shops (Fixed Assets £13,000, less net capital £8,500)   4,500
   (all to be used to reduce its trade creditors) and
   (b) to purchase the fixed assets of Square Plate Company at valuation (Goodwill £3,000 plus Shops and Fittings £7,300)   10,300

   the minimum increase required in fixed capital was, say... £15,000

2. The bank manager ascertained that: £

   (a) The private resources of Mr. Bull outside the company
      included his residence, with a minimum equity of
      £4,000, quoted shares after margin £3,500, and a life
      policy with a surrender value of £500. Total   8,000

   (b) The two shops to be bought from the Square Plate
      Company could be mortgaged for at least   4,000

   (c) One shop belonging to China Shops Ltd. was free and
      could be mortgaged for   3,000

   (d) The earning capacity of the combined businesses was
      undoubtedly adequate to meet mortgage reductions
      and permit of surplus profits for the gradual accumu-   ————
      lation of adequate working capital £15,000

3. It was therefore agreed that to enable China Shops Ltd. to
complete its purchase of the Dish business for £10,000 and
to settle trade creditors, say £4,500, the bank would
immediately lend up to   15,000
to be secured by a legal mortgage on all the free shops, set
out above, worth, say £7,000
and a second mortgage on the other shops (for
what worth) plus the collateral security of the
assets of Mr. Bull, valued at £8,000
                                    ————
                                    15,000

on the strict understanding that within two months the
outside mortgages would be completed to yield............   7,000
and Mr. Bull would mortgage his residence for............   4,000
lending the proceeds to the company on fixed term.   ————
                                    £11,000

thereby reducing the bank overdraft to £4,000 secured by the collateral
shares and life policy worth £4,000 and the second mortgages on the
original properties. Mr. Bull undertook to reduce any remaining bank
advances from profits by not less than £500 per annum.

In view of the comparitively negligible total of current assets, Mr.
Cashe did not think it prudent to seek a floating charge as additional
security. He was impressed with the business capacity (but not the financial
acumen) of Mr. Bull and content to rely on future profits to improve the
position. Finally to prove that the arrangements were satisfactory, Mr.
Cashe drew up the following estimate of the combined position after all
the mortgages had been obtained, and applied the gone concern test.

	£		£	Forced Sale Estimate £
Net Capital	4,500	Goodwill	3,000	—
Mortgages (£4,000 plus £7,000)	11,000	Shops (all mortgaged) and ten-		
Fixed Loan from Mr. Bull (mortgage of		ancies	16,800	11,000
residence)	4,000	Fixtures & Fittings	2,000	—
		Motors	1,500	1,000
Total Fixed Capital	19,500			
H.P. Creditors (on motors)	1,000	Total Fixed Assets	23,300	
Trade Creditors (£7,300 plus £2,500		Stock	5,700 ⎫	
minus £4,500)	5,300	Trade Debtors (hotels—other	⎬ 4,000	
Bank Advance	4,000	sales for cash)	500 ⎭	
		Cash in hand	300	—
	29,800		29,800	16,000

After satisfying the mortgage and hire purchase creditiors, only £4,000 remained on this worst basis to meet unsecured creditors £13,300, including the bank £4,000, and the likely dividend upon failure amounted to say 30p in £, leaving a risk of £2,800. In view of the good collateral security, worth £4,000, the manager did not ask Mr. Bull to postpone his loan to the claims of the bank.

Weary, but with a sense of achievement, Mr. Cashe retired for a well-earned luncheon. The details of his exploits may well be criticised, but the principles are clear.

3. *Overtrading illustrated.*

Returning refreshed from the luncheon interval, the imaginary Mr. Cashe finds his equally fictitious decorator acquaintance, Mr. Slapdash, anxiously awaiting him. As sole proprietor of the R.A. Beautifying Company, this customer has hitherto borrowed up to £500 against a life policy worth the same amount, but he now hastens to explain that he needs a further £1,500 at once to pay the weekly wages of his workmen. He is heavily engaged on important large-scale housing sub-contracts and the unexpected delay in the receipt of progress payments for work done has left him temporarily short of cash. Whilst no other security is available, the bank can be assured that moneys will soon be received from debtors to restore the position, and to prove his point Mr. Slapdash produces the following figures extracted from his books by a local accoutant at the end of the previous week.

LIABILITIES	£	ASSETS	£
Trade Creditors	9,300	Ladders, etc.	200
Capital	1,000	Stock of paint	600
		Work-in-progress	6,300
		Debtors	500
		Retentions	2,700
	10,300		10,300

Mr. Cashe is appalled to find that, with working capital £800, this customer has £2,700 frozen in retention moneys and £6,300 in work-in-progress. He is relying entirely on the prompt receipt of progress payments to meet wages and pressing creditors, whilst happily taking on more and more large contracts at fine prices hoping that trade creditors will wait until retentions can be collected. Mr Slapdash emphasised the demand for his work, the contracts to come, the pressure upon his staff and the profits he is making, but the prudent and experienced manager is not impressed. This is a patent case of gross overtrading and it is remarkable that the balloon has been kept at such high pressure without bursting. The pin is now poised for the fatal prick and, unless the customer can attract capital or collect sufficient immediately from debtors, the collapse is inevitable. It is already too late to preach caution and the contention that the assets are undoubted in value can be of no avail. However unsympathetic he may appear to be and despite the protestations of the customer, Mr. Cashe has no alternative but to regret the inability of the bank to find the money.

The day of our imaginary manager and this review of balance sheets must, therefore, end on an unhappy but salutory note.

The Trading and Profit and Loss Account

The basic principles of lending demand, *inter alia,* that the banker should have confidence in the ability and experience of the potential borrower and should be able to trace with reasonable certainty the source from which repayment of the proposed advance will be made. In the case of a trading customer, the success or otherwise of past trading is clearly revealed in the trading and profit and loss accounts which usually accompany the balance sheet when it is produced for the perusal of the banker, and the net profits made in recent years provide an indication of what should be available to reduce the borrowing from the bank. The extent of the information disclosed will vary considerably from the exhaustive detailed private accounts, with innumerable schedules, specially rendered for the complete guidance of the bank to the published figures of a public limited company which merely reveal the bare facts required by the Companies Act. If the situation so demands, the bank can always call for more detailed figures for its purpose. If these figures are studied and compared with previous trading years, any unusual features can be discussed with the customer and a wealth of information thereby obtained to guide the bank. The need to read the balance sheet in conjunction with the accompanying trading and profit and loss account has already been explained in connection with the analysis of the creditors, debtors, and stock items. It is now prudent to mention the chief points demanding attention in a standard trading profit and loss account, including comparison with the figures for previous years.

TRADING RESULTS

The primary test is to ascertain the earning capacity of the business under review and to explore any major fluctuations in profits in recent trading periods, always comparing like with like. A standard has to be adopted for general use, distinguishing clearly between the following three measures of profit:

1. *Gross Profit.*
The method of determining gross profit may vary slightly with different types of business, but basically it is the profit made after charging only those costs which are directly incurred in the given production and/or sales of the goods or services of the business. Broadly speaking, all costs

which vary directly with the turnover and directly affect the prime cost of the goods or services are charged to the trading or manufacturing account, which is credited with the proceeds of sales, and the net result is the gross profit earned before all other charges which appear in the profit and loss account.

2. *Net Corporation Tax.*

The final profit figure after charging all the costs of the business, including taxation provisions but before any transfers are made to reserves or dividends are paid, is the net profit. This figure cannot always be picked out automatically from the profit and loss account because taxation frequently appears in the profit and loss appropriation account and the picture is confused because capital profits, balances carried forward and dividend entries also appear in the appropriation account. Exceptional non-trading receipts must naturally be excluded by the bank from the net profit figure to maintain the standard for comparison purposes. A profit figure can obviously be unduly swollen or a loss wiped out by a profit made on the sale of certain fixed assets, but it will be a non-recurring receipt which must be excluded to determine the earning capacity of the business. It is, therefore, often necessary to extract the net profit figure by arithmetical process, deducting from the final profit figure in the profit and loss account items such as directors' fees, taxation and sometimes depreciation, appearing in the appropriation account and adding back or deducting, as the case may be, any exceptional receipts or debits which would destroy the true trading picture.

3. *Net Profit before Tax and Depreciation and Interest Charges.*

This final standard gives the real earning capacity of the business and for comparison purposes removes the distortion which may arise from variations in the rates of taxation. Directors' fees or proprietors' salaries can also be added back to the net profit figure so that the results record the actual profit made in the trading period before anything is drawn by the proprietors and before payment of taxation and provision for depreciation. Nowadays, taxation represents such a heavy cost that it is essential to decide the profit capacity before tax, although the surplus available for reducing the bank debt will be after payment of taxation. On the other hand, amounts charged for depreciation do not reduce the cash surplus available for reductions. Interest paid on loans, mortgages, debentures or bank borrowing may also be added back to reach this standard profit figure on the grounds that it is the price paid for capital resources and not a true trading cost.

Whichever standard is adopted, it is essential always to follow it closely for comparison purposes, otherwise the picture will be distorted and useless as a guide to the bank. Usually all three standards are adopted and the trading results scheduled in such manner that they can be compared over the years at a glance. Major fluctuations, unusual items and apparent extravagances call for comment and may need to be explored with the customers and, having distinguished between the main profit standards, features of particualr interest to the banker can now be discussed.

A start can always be made with the sales figure for the period under review. How does it compare with the total for previous periods? Have sales increased in keeping with general trade conditions or have they fallen unexpectedly? In the latter event, what has caused the reduction? Is the customer meeting increased competition or is there some weakness in the management or sales organisation? If the fall in sales cannot be arrested, difficulties will arise; what steps are the proprietors taking to increase sales? It may be a temporary setback experienced by all customers in the same line of business, or it may be exceptional in the case of the particular borrower. What are the prospects for the future?

Any material increase in advertising expenditure or in travellers' salaries, etc., shown in the profit and loss account should be reflected in larger sales in the trading account unless prices have been cut to increase the turnover of goods. There is often a clear link between such items. Steadily increasing sales year by year are a healthy sign and, providing all costs are properly controlled, should result in *pro rata* increases in profits before tax and depreciation. If not, the figures demand closer scrutiny to decide the causes, which may have to be explored with the customer. Where sales increase materially but profits nevertheless fall, there may be carelessness in the control of outgoings which needs tightening up in the future. On all such points the bank manager must naturally be sure of his facts before raising comment with the customer as the bank cannot normally interfere in the conduct of the business unless it is clear that the weaknesses disclosed by the figures are jeopardising the bank's position. Generally, the sales figures should be recorded and compared over the years in relation to the gross profit and net profit for each trading year.

The gross profit next demands consideration. How does it compare with previous years? Does it rise and fall *pro rata* with sales? If not, is there any satisfactory explanation? Wage rates may have been increased without any adjustment in selling prices or the method of valuing stock may have been changed. There may be errors in the valuation of stock or sale prices may have been cut to meet competition. The ratio of gross profit to sales expressed as a percentage of sales can often be compared with the gross profit ratio of similar types of business and undue variations explored. The gross profit ratio of customers retailing standard goods, sweets and tobacco, grocers, butchers, etc., should show little variation, but with larger concerns producing or marketing specialised products no valid comparison can be drawn. On the other hand, an unduly small gross profit ratio may call for comment unless there is a large turnover yielding a satisfactory gross profit. Fluctuations in gross profit can, of course, result from changes in the policy of the proprietors by charging against sales in the trading account costs which were previously debited to profit and loss account.

Before leaving the trading account, it is well to remind readers that the trade debtors figure in the balance sheet should be compared with the sales for the period to ensure that, on average, outstanding debtors are reasonable and undue credit is not being granted to buyers. The incidence of seasonal fluctuations or other unusual features applying to the business under review may have to be taken into account. In like manner, the trade creditors figure in the balance sheet is compared with the total purchases debited to the trading account to verify that the business is not taking unduly long credit from its suppliers. Finally, the stock figure should be compared with the total sales for the period and an average taken to ensure that, with due regard to any seasonal features, the stock on hand is reasonable in relation to the normal requirements of the business. These simple tests have all been explained but are repeated here for the sake of emphasis.

A study of the items debited and credited to the profit and loss account will then complete the banker's picture of the trading of the borrower. If need be, they can also be scheduled in detail and compared over the years. Any undue fluctuation or unusual items may call for explanation according to the degree of risk accepted by the bank in granting the overdraft facilities under review. For example, the amount written-off in respect of bad debts may be relatively large. Is it an isolated instance of failure of a large buyer or is it due to laxity in granting credit? There may be relatively heavy charges for monies borrowed privately or for hire purchase facilities. Are they justified from the bank's standpoint in relation to the remainder of the picture? How much has been spent on extraneous expenses, such as travelling, entertaining, car upkeep, etc? Are such costs reasonable in relation to profits? Tactful criticism may be required from the bank where profits are small and the bank account is conducted in an unsatisfactory manner. Throughout, the depth of the bank's analysis of the items and the extent of any criticism will depend on the size and soundness of the bank advance in relation to the net profits of the borrower. There can be no fixed rule in practice and, with a satisfactory customer earning reasonable profits, it would be unwise to raise comments which might suggest that the bank is attempting to interfere in the conduct of the customer's business. Where losses occur or profits are negligible through apparent extravagancies or weak management and the bank's position is in jeopardy, it is a vastly different story. Prompt action must be taken and undertakings obtained from the customers to correct their ways, otherwise the bank advance may have to be called in. The point is that many such weaknesses first come to light from an intelligent survey of the trading and profit and loss figures. For example, a rental item appearing for the first time on the credit side of the profit and loss account may reveal that, unknown to the bank, the customer has leased a part of his factory or other building over which the bank has a legal mortgage. Why is such space no longer required in the customer's business and what effect has this lease had upon the bank's security?

Finally, the profit and loss appropriation account demands study to decide whether a reasonable proportion of the profits are being retained in the business to reduce bank borrowing and/or to provide for future contingencies. Nothing can be more disconcerting than to find that, despite the anxiety of the bank for reductions, the proprietors have withdrawn by way of dividend in the case of a limited company or by way of partners' drawings from a firm, the major portion of the profits earned in the period. Sometimes, for example, the amount paid away in preference dividend may exceed the net profit earned by the limited company customer. Such features call for comment. In the more prudently managed concern there will be reasonable transfers to reserves and the amount ultimately paid away in dividends will be limited to a portion only of the net profits. The figures will be self-explanatory and can be criticised or applauded in relation to the given facts. The point is that they should be studied and understood by the branch banker, who is in direct contact with the borrower. A word of caution or a helpful suggestion at the right moment can do much to protect the bank's position and should foster goodwill with the customer who normally will appreciate the close interest of the bank. Excessive payments to shareholders or partners obviously reduce the cash available to fund any bank debt, but the proprietors of the business and not the bank are expected to shoulder the risk and should be the last to participate in the profits which have been made.

The Limited Company Profit and Loss Account.
Before leaving this subject, it may be helpful to summarise the disclosure required by law in the profit and loss account of a limited company. Section 148 of the Companies Act, 1948, requires that the directors of every company shall at some date not later than eighteen months after the incorporation of the company and subsequently once at least in every calendar year lay before the company in general meeting a profit and loss account, or in the case of a company not trading for profit, an income and expenditure account for the period, in the case of the first account, since the incorporation of the company, and, in any other case, since the preceding account made up to a date not earlier than the date of the meeting by more than nine months, or in the case of a company carrying on business or having interests abroad by more than twelve months. Every profit and loss account has to furnish a true and fair view of the

profit or loss of the company for the financial year and, *alia*, the following details must be disclosed to comply with the Eighth Schedule of the Companies Act, 1948 (as amended by Schedule 1 of the Companies Act 1967).

(*a*)   the amount charged to revenue by way of provision for depreciation, renewals or diminution in value of fixed assets;

(*b*)   the amount of the interest on loans of the following kinds made to the company whether on the security of debentures or not, namely bank loans, overdrafts and loans which are not bank loans or overdrafts but

    (i)   are repayable otherwise by instalments and fall due for repayment before the expiration of the period of five years beginning with the day next following the expiration of the financial year; or

    (ii)   are repayable by instalments the last of which falls due for payment before the expiration of that period,

and the amount of interest on loans of other kinds so made.

(*c*)   the amount of the charge to revenue for United Kingdom corporation tax and, if that amount would have been greater but for relief from double taxation, the amount it would have been but for such relief the amount of the charge for United Kingdom tax and the amount of the charge for taxation imposed outside the United Kingdom of profits, income and (so far as charged to revenue) capital gains;

(*d*)   the amounts respectively provided for redemption of share capital and for redemption of loans;

(*e*)   the amount, if material, set aside or proposed to be set aside to, or withdrawn from reserves;

(*f*)   the amount, if material, set aside to provisions other than provisions for depreciation, renewals or diminution in value of assets or, as the case may be, the amount, if material, withdrawn from such provisions and not applied for the purposes thereof;

(*g*)   the amounts respectively of income from quoted investments and income from unquoted investments;

(*h*)   if a substantial part of the company's revenue for the financial year consists in rents from land, the amount thereof, after deduction of ground rents, rates and other outgoings;

(*i*)   the amount, if material, charged to revenue in respect of sums payable in respect of the hire of plant and machinery;

(*j*)   the aggregate amount of the dividends paid and proposed.

Moreover, the aggregate amount of the directors' emoluments, pensions and any compensation to directors in respect of loss of office have to be shown separately. (See Section 196 of the 1948 Act for full details.) This provision may be helpful to the banker where the directors are in fact drawing an undue share of the earnings of the company.

COMPARISON OF FIGURES

The analysis of the balance sheet and trading and profit and loss account of any customer on the lines explained throughout these pages is invaluable as so much can be gleaned to guide the lending banker. A comparison of the principal figures over the years is even more helpful because major fluctuations can be seen at a glance and their impact on the position quickly appreciated. The importance of such a comparison is recognised at law in that Clause 11 (11) of the Eighth Schedule of the Companies Act, 1948, requires that the balance sheet of a company shall show the corresponding amounts at the end of the immediately preceding financial year for all items shown in the balance sheet. The figures for two years can, therefore, always be seen and compared in the published balance sheet of a limited company.

The method of comparison may vary in detail, but the principles are the same. It is essential to compare like with like. For example, it would be senseless to compare the figures for a trading year with those for the previous six months, or to compare interim balance sheet figures with the final balance sheet where seasonal features apply to the business. No doubt most banks record the balance sheet figures of customers on standard lines so that the total current liabilities and the main items comprised therein are listed each year in the same order and can be compared by reading across the columns. If the fixed capital divided appropriately between loan capital and proprietors' capital including reserves is likewise summarised, the comparison is a simple matter. The assets can also be scheduled, perhaps in order of realisability, with a sub-total for the floating assets to facilitate a quick assessment of the liquid position of the borrower. Finally, the main profit and loss items can be scheduled to record the progress or otherwise of the business. The interpretation of such comparative schedules is then a matter of common sense and the principles can perhaps best be explained by reference to the following imaginary practical example.

Northtown Bank lends £10,000 on overdraft to its customer XYZ Ltd. and, as the account has recently been working heavily, the manager thinks it well to revise his knowledge of the recent financial history of these customers. His records show the following summary position for the past few years and the manager has no difficulty in interpreting what has happened from the scheduled figures.

What a tale these figures unfold. The business has made good progress with increased sales at a steady gross profit ratio, but final results are disappointing because relatively heavy emoluments are paid to the directors and the cash margin for the reduction of bank borrowing is not large having regard to the heavy secured creditors whose interest charges have also to be met. Can nothing be done to economise on overheads to improve the net profit figures? The acquisition of fixed assets over these years has been financed from fresh capital and long-term borrowing. The net increase of £12,500 in the value of the company's shops and buildings has been more than covered by increased long-term borrowing (mortgages are up by £6,000 and there are now debentures £10,000), whilst there

X Y Z Limited
(Wholesale and retail chemists and fancy goods)

Balance Sheet as at:	31.12.74	31.12.75	31.12.76	31.12.77
LIABILITIES	£	£	£	£
Trade Creditors	12,700	13,200	18,000	19,500
Due to subsidiaries	—	—	4,500	8,000
Taxation	1,300	1,900	2,400	2,600
Dividend payable	600	600	1,200	1,200
Bank debt	1,800	19,000	4,000	16,000
Total current liabilities:	16,400	34,700	30,100	47,300
5% Debentures	—	—	10,000	10,000
Mortgages	4,000	6,000	10,000	10,000
Fixed Loans	—	—	3,000	1,000
	20,400	40,700	53,100	68,300
Capital	12,000	12,000	24,000	24,000
Reserves	4,000	6,000	500	2,000
Profit & Loss A/c	—	1,500	1,800	1,500
Total	34,600	60,200	79,400	95,800
ASSETS				
Cash	100	400	300	700
Trade Debtors	6,000	8,500	9,500	15,000
Stock	10,100	34,400	26,200	37,600
Total floating assets:	16,200	43,300	36,000	53,300
Shops & Buildings	8,500	8,000	22,400	21,000
Fixtures & Fittings	3,000	2,500	7,000	7,500
Motors, etc.	1,700	2,400	5,000	6,000
Investments in Subsidiaries	—	—	6,000	6,000
Goodwill	5,000	4,000	3,000	2,000
Profit & Loss A/c	2,000	—	—	—
Total	36,400	60,200	79,400	95,800
Sales	100,000	126,000	130,000	145,000
Gross Profit	29,000	37,800	40,300	43,500
Ratio of Gross Profit to Sales	29%	30%	31%	30%
Directors	4,000	4,000	6,000	7,500
Bad Debts	3,150	400	1,600	1,800
Interest Charges	275	1,250	1,600	2,000
Depreciation	500	1,000	2,000	2,500
Taxation	3,000	4,600	3,900	4,250
Net profit or loss:	Loss 1,400	P.6,100	P.2,000	P.2,400
Dividends Paid	600	600	1,200	1,200
To Reserves	—	2,000	500	1,500

has been an increase of £13,500 in the actual capital resources of the company. Clearly when the company bought new premises and acquired an interest in a subsidiary in 1976 the capital was doubled by a cash issue of £6,000 and a transfer of £6,000 from reserve, whilst mortgages were increased by £4,000 and £10,000 was borrowed against debentures. In other words, a prudent financial policy was adopted and the liquid position of the company remained undisturbed, leaving the bank to finance occasional requirements for normal trading. Debtors have increased with increased sales, but stock is heavy in relation to sales and has in fact been excessive in the past three years. As the company has entered into no fresh capital commitment, it may be that the recent heavy overdraft tendency results from heavy stock purchases, and the manager decides to explore the current stock position.

In short, the general financial history of XYZ Ltd. is clearly painted on a canvas for the experienced banker to interpret. Many other conclusions can be drawn according to the imagination of the reader, but lest the example be subject to expert criticism, it may be as well to add that, in view of the heavy secured creditors, the bank holds undoubted collateral security worth £8,000 to support the borrowing.

The general purpose and method of comparison of these figures having been illustrated, this serial story of all the lessons and guidance which the prudent banker can obtain from an intelligent survey of a customer's balance sheet and trading and profit and loss account can now be brought to an end. The joy of lending is surely in the correct appreciation of the risk, and the satisfaction derived from affording assistance to a worthy, although not necessarily wealthy, customer is unbounded. The art of assessing a lending proposal from all aspects, including the interpretation of the balance sheet position, develops with practical experience, and the principles outlined herein serve only as an introduction to a subject which has no bounds and subscribes to no rigid rules, being subject to the dictates of policy and expediency in the best interests of healthy competition.

Chapter XII

Formalised Personal Lending Services

The great advantage of the British banking overdraft system is the flexibility it offers to the personal customer in the use of the limited facility provided by the bank and the ease and informality with which the loan can be repaid or extended. Formalised lending schemes are administered in a predetermined and relatively inflexible way so that customer "buys" a "packaged" facility fully aware of how he must take the loan and in due course repay. Clearly the advantage to the clearing bank is the ease of administration; the systems are easily conveyed to thousands of branch managers and staff and the "packages" lend themselves to mass marketing. Lastly, formalised systems are particularly easy to administer using credit scoring techniques which can be applied by staff without a wide knowledge or experience of personal lending generally.

It is impossible to cover the variety of schemes introduced by banks since 1958; some have been successful others have failed to register public interest. A selection of the main types of formalised lending schemes are mentioned below, but it must be emphasized that the aggregate of these types of loans is small in relation to the totality of clearing bank lending and that these are exceptions to the general rule that bank advances are repayable on demand.

PERSONAL LOANS

In 1958 Midland Bank introduced its personal loan service. Many other banks quickly followed with similar schemes providing the public with a cheaper form of borrowing to meet personal capital outlay, repayable in agreed instalments over a reasonable period. Whilst these schemes varied in detail, they all followed the same basic pattern. During the intervening years despite the severe credit restrictions placed upon personal borrowing from banks the schemes have become well established, in fact the title has been absorbed into the vernacular as a common reference to personal lending of any description.

PURPOSES OF LOAN

The scheme is devised to assist a customer to meet exceptional non-recurring items of expenditure. The purpose of such advances is not limited to the purchase of domestic appliances and furniture, motor cars and motor cycles, but includes home repairs, decorations, improvements and the education of children. Whilst primarily limited to personal customers the facilities may be made available in exceptional cases to cover the capital requirements of small one-man businesses and partnerships, and professional men may be able to borrow to finance their purchase of appliances and furniture. The purpose of the advance can, therefore, vary to a wide extent, but it must be a reasonable requirement within the standard of living and creditworthiness of the borrower.

AMOUNT OF THE LOAN

The amount of any personal loan has naturally to be considered in relation to the purpose for which it is required and the means of the customer. As ever, prudence demands that the borrower should provide from his or her own resources a reasonable deposit or proportion of the total proposed outlay. The general scheme provides for loans ranging from a minimum of £50, increasing to a maximum of £2,000. In approved circumstances this maximum may be exceeded.

COST TO BORROWER

Instead of calculating interest half-yearly on the daily debit balance, the interest is calculated at the published rate for the entire term of the loan and added to the principal debt when the advance is taken. The rate charged on loans already taken will remain unchanged throughout the life of the loan. The borrower thus knows the full extent of his commitent at the outset and the bank accepts the risk that money rates may rise materially during the period of the advance.

Although the full amount of interest is added to the loan at the beginning, the bank can only take into its profits the proportion of interest actually paid during the trading year. All repayments have, therefore, to be divided into capital and interest instalments. This need inevitably complicates the book-keeping and increases the labour cost involved in providing the service, although in many instances this process has now been computerised.

REPAYMENT

The borrower is required to liquidate the entire debt within a maximum period of three years in equal monthly instalments, but shorter periods from six to thirty months can be arranged to suit individual circumstances. The borrower thus knows exactly how much has to be found on an agreed date in each month, and the actual payment entails no trouble or additional expense because it is transferred by the bank from the current account of the customer to the personal loan account in accord with standing instructions. The form of agreement signed by the customer when negotiating the loan includes a clause authorising the bank to debit the current account each month with the required instalment. This relieves the customer of the trouble of remembering to pay each instalment as it falls due. It is all very simple, providing sufficient cash is available in the current account to meet the monthly instalment.

A special feature of many of these schemes is that, in the unhappy event of the death of the customer before the loan has been liquidated, the banks do not expect repayment of the outstanding balance. The loan is automatically discharged and no liability for repayment rests with the deceased's estate. This is a great attraction to any borrower, particularly one with family commitments.

SECURED PERSONAL LOANS

The success of the unsecured facility encouraged the banks to extend the scheme to cover larger purchases or financial commitments—extensions to houses, constructing a garage, supporting university or private school education. Where borrowing up to £5,000 or more was contemplated the immediate ability of the borrower to repay had to be considered against the size of the loan, the possible future incapacity of the customer or the likelihood of his loss of employment. The availability of security, perhaps by way of a second mortgage on a house or by charging a life policy enabled the bank to extend a formalised lending facility beyond the limits of the previously determined unsecured service.

BUDGET ACCOUNT

Few people enjoy a situation where outgoings form a regular pattern in line with weekly or monthly income. Public utility accounts are usually rendered on a quarterly basis and rates are charged half-yearly. Although arrangements can be made to make such payments monthly, this is often costly and not always convenient. Many banks offer budget account facilities enabling personal customers to aggregate their expected annual outgoings and divided by twelve pay the bank a total monthly sum. This is credited to a special account out of which the designated bills are paid as and when required. It follows this account will swing from credit to debit and if the sums have been correctly estimated reduce to nil over the twelve months period. Charges are made for setting up the account and for each withdrawal as well as interest allowed or paid on the daily balances produced. This form of budgeting has proved very popular.

REVOLVING CREDIT

Not all customers are certain about their requirements for fixed term borrowing so that a personal loan may not be immediately convenient. Over the years bank managers have watched borrowers take and repay a succession of personal loans. The application of a revolving credit scheme is to first class credit risks and forms the basis for a continuous personal loan.

A separate loan account is provided with a maximum limit for indebtedness. The customer undertakes to provide monthly payments of a fixed sum by way of standing order instructions to the debit of his current account. The limit for borrowing is an agreed multiple of the monthly payment. It is now up to the customer to utilise the loan by means of transfers to his current account. It follows that the revolving credit account may swing between credit and debit depending upon usage and interest is allowed or charged by the bank accordingly.

While there is a risk for "hardcore" or semi-permanent lending to arise control of the facility by the banker is relatively simple and careful credit assessment before approval will normally provide a carefree lending situation.

Credit cards are used principally for routine payments in stores, hotels, garages, restaurants, railway stations and even airports. A simple, un-encoded plastic card contains only a specimen signature of the holder but is embossed with details of his name, card number and its expiry date, which can be transferred to an accounting voucher, already imprinted with the retailer's details, by means of a simple, hand operated machine.

The retailer can obtain immediate credit to his current account by "paying-in" these credit card vouchers over a bank counter. The vouchers are remitted to the credit card company's central "factory" where the cardholder's account is debited. Accounts are then rendered to cardholders by way of a monthly statement, which advises the last date for settlement when interest will be charged on the outstanding debt for the whole period of indebtedness. While many users find full settlement within the period allowed a cheap and easy method for making payments, others find the use of the credit available a convenient way to finance irregular outlays on consumer goods.

Credit card companies derive income from interest earned on cardholders' loans and discounts payable by retailers on purchases made by the users of the schemes. This duality of income gives rise to a popular misconception that the two bank-owned card companies provide funds themselves to finance their lending operations. In fact the banks include these loans within their total personal advances, thus ensuring that the lending is covered by the normal liquidity considerations and, when applicable, official constraints on finance for personal consumption.

ADVANTAGES OF THE FORMALISED SCHEMES

From the standpoint of the customer in need of assistance the range of services available provide convenient and attractive methods of borrowing. There are few formalities beyond the completion of an application form or a frank discussion with a bank official; the charges are competitive with hire purchase or other forms of point-of-sale finance.

For those facing the problem of meeting a capital purchase or other form of non-recurring lump sum payment the fixed-term personal loan provides a known monthly payment from the outset covering both principal and interest. Should the customer's requirements be less certain a revolving credit facility with a bank gives him the option to draw down the loan as he requires the funds, retaining the fixed monthly payment but with an opportunity to save as well as to borrow to fit his circumstances and his needs. The credit card, as well as being a simple and convenient way of making routine payments at home and abroad, fulfils the desires, perhaps too readily in some cases, of the impulse buyer with the knowledge that a credit limit is available to finance monthly purchases by way of a revolving credit facility. In this case the size of monthly repayment can be varied by borrower above the statutory minimum of £5 or 5 per cent. of the outstanding balance.

Another important but unofficial feature is that in all these instances, including the use of a credit card, the customer is dealing with his bank which should know him well and, if unexpected hardship intervenes through sickness or other unavoidable adversity, it is probable that he will find the bank more sympathetic and reasonable over the question of the payment of instalments than a lender who is a stranger holding security on the asset acquired on an instalment basis. The schemes do not provide for deferred payment of the agreed instalments, but where misfortune intervenes through no fault of the customer no doubt temporary accommodation will be granted exceptionally on the current account of the borrower to meet the repayments. This is a factor which may arise out of the normal banker and customer relationship in isolated cases of hardship where, despite the precautions taken at the outset, the finance budget of the borrower has been completely upset by an unexpected development quite beyond his control. It is an advantage which cannot be advertised, but no doubt it will be recognised by customers who have confidence in their banker.

Providing the facilities are properly controlled by branch managers, formalised personal lending schemes can be of considerable benefit to the banks. By thus widening the range of the lending services, the banks are providing approved customers with a convenient and more simple means of finance which should attract many new customers from the ranks of those who have hitherto felt no need for a banking account. Every facility normally calls for a current account to service it and anyone attracted initially into the bank by the possibility of obtaining a loan can quickly be made to realise the other advantages of maintaining a current account for normal payments. The schemes should therefore, encourage the growth of banking accounts by attracting fresh customers. With a close knowledge of the financial position, general standing and integrity of a customer based on experience over a period, the banks have long been in a position to judge the creditworthiness of an individual without the need for outside status enquiries and financial reports and repayments can be collected in a simple and inexpensive manner under standing instructions.

The rates charged on each scheme have varied with economic conditions and the ebb and flow of costs in the money market. The actual return to the lending bank has always been considerably higher than the yield on overdraft, but allowance has to be made for the fixed-term nature of the loan, provided monthly repayments are maintained, the greater risk of bad debts and in many cases, the interest rate to be applied throughout being agreed when the funds are first taken by the borrower. From the Banks' point of view, however, the risks are very well spread over many advances, each for a relatively small amount, and if due care is exercised, bad debts should be negligible. Much obviously depends upon the branch manager entrusted with the responsibility of granting or refusing requests for personal finance and an attempt can now be made to survey the points which have to be considered by the branch banker when negotiating such a facility with a customer.

BASIC PRINCIPLES OF LENDING APPLIED

From the standpoint of the practical banker, no fresh principles emerge in providing these personal services, which are normally routine unsecured lending. Fundamentally, there is no difference in principle, but the schemes undoubtedly attract many fresh borrowers and, with an increased demand for loans, branch officers have much more opportunity to exercise their judgment and resource, applying the basic canons of lending to far more proposals than they have previously been called upon to examine. There should be an increased awareness of the need for a finance budget to be supplied by the private customer and examined and criticised by the banker. With no security normally taken in support, the responsibility of the lending banker is clearly increased. All the facts have to be collated to enable the manager to appreciate the risk and to decide whether or not to grant the loan. Without such a meticulous appreciation, blind lending will result with repayment left to chance, constituting bad banking. What information will normally be required and how can the banker best assess the position? It is merely a question of applying the basic principles of lending to each proposal. Above all, the loan must be "safe", being granted to an undoubted, able borrower who can repay by the agreed instalments over the approved period from known sources. The "liquidity" of the advance and its "profitability" are thus assured within the basic scheme. With the removal of credit restrictions, the problem of the "suitability" of the advance is limited to banking policy and easily decided when the purpose of the requirement is ascertained. Nevertheless, in order to be satisfied that a proposal generally fulfils these basic canons of good lending, many factors have to be considered and an attempt can be made to follow the thoughts of a branch manager interviewing a customer who is applying for a personal loan.

1. THE BORROWER

To be safe the loan must clearly be granted to a borrower in whom the lender may have every confidence. According to the special advertisement of one bank furnishing this service, it is based upon the personal integrity of its customers and not upon the material security which they can provide. It is common knowledge that a good banker should know his customer and be able to judge not only his integrity but his ability to use the bank money to advantage and to repay it within an acceptable period. Who then is the borrower and what does the banker know of his business experience and integrity? What are the nature and prospects of his business or employment in relation to economic conditions? Is he credit-worthy?

What is known of the experience of the borrower? By whom is he employed and upon what terms? If a private trader or partner in a firm, has he made a success of the business to date? How long has he been engaged in this particular trade and what profits has he earned? Does he normally spend all his income or does he live prudently, leaving adequate margin for contingencies? Does he enjoy good health and possess drive and energy with ample capacity for hard work? Has he a reasonable financial acumen or is he unduly optimistic and attempting too much in order perhaps to satisfy a personal craving for an article beyond his standing of living? Every bank manager should know his customers and from contact and local knowledge be aware of their experience, capacity and temperament, to assess their creditworthiness. In many cases the salary of an employee customer will be credited monthly to his account and his commitments by way of life policy premiums, building society repayments, hire purchase instalments and other outgoings will be patent from an examination of the account. The information is often readily available from this source. If the manager has no confidence in the integrity and financial capacity of the customer, the only problem will be to decide how best to decline the loan in a tactful manner without loss of other credit business.

2. PURPOSE OF THE ADVANCE

A general indication of the purposes for which such loans can be obtained has already been given, but the desirability of the purpose has always to be considered in relation to the known standard of living, resources and surplus net income of the potential borrower. Any extravagance or attempt to acquire articles which are not essential should clearly be dis-couraged. There is little point in financing the purchase of a car when it is obvious from the finance budget that, although the customer may be able to repay the loan, the strain of running and maintaining the car would be unduly heavy in relation to income. Prudence demands that the purpose should be reasonable and that the manager should be ready to advise against unnecessary or extravagant outlay. There is no question of competition with other lenders on hire purchase terms to encourage customers to indulge in capital spending which is beyond their income, and it is incumbent upon the bank manager to keep a fatherly eye on this aspect in the best interests of the customer as well as of the bank.

3. AMOUNT REQUIRED

The amount required has to be examined not only in relation to the capital resources, income, and existing financial commitments of the borrower, but also in relation to the purpose for which the personal loan is wanted. It obviously must be sufficient when added to the deposit or proportion found by the customer to complete the purchase or commitment in question. Moreover, the borrower should be able to make a reasonable contribution to the outlay from his existing resources, borrowing from the bank only a part of the total actually required. It is definitely not the function of the bank to find the entire amount required. The extent of the stake introduced by the borrower will vary according to the circumstances and some banks have adopted the current hire purchase practices as a loose guide to the minimum deposit expected. This is mere business prudence in the best interests of the customer which does not destroy the value of the service to the reliable customer. No definite rule can be laid down because the amount of the deposit required will necessarily vary according to all the other factors under consideration, but a customer cannot expect the bank to provide the entire amount needed to finance his outlay.

Furthermore, in many cases it may be wise to follow the application of the proceeds of the advance. If the amount lent on personal loan is credited to the general account of the customer, it should be possible to trace the payment made therefrom to achieve the given purpose. Everything naturally depends upon the integrity of the customer, but with personal loans, money advanced for a certain purpose must unquestionably be used for that purpose and not converted to meet other needs. There is no legal link-up and, unless the bank intervenes to pay direct to the supplier, it has to rely upon the customer. Production of the paid account of the supplier may perhaps be advisable in isolated cases. Generally speaking, however, if a customer can be entrusted with an unsecured loan he can be relied upon to apply the money in keeping with his contract with the bank.

4. REPAYMENT

Finally, the reliability of the source of repayment has to be examined to ensure the liquidity of the loan. The source will normally be from surplus income which may be earned or unearned, or both. In any event, the income is subject to tax, to any prior charges and to essential living expenses. The length of the advance will vary up to a maximum of three years and borrowers should be discouraged from undue optimism in attempting to repay too rapidly. The amount of the monthly instalment must be reasonable in relation to proved surplus income, after due allowance for contingencies. A personal finance budget compiled perhaps by question and answer between banker and customer is the complete solution. The sureness of the income, ignoring all doubtful extras, can be ascertained and personal expenditure assessed prudently on a monthly basis, including all standing commitments and reserves for sickness, holidays, etc. In many cases the optimism of the customer will be unlimited and it will then be incumbent upon the bank manager to preach caution, suggesting perhaps that the borrower might defer the outlay until he can accumulate a larger initial deposit, thereby reducing the extent of the loan and the amount required each month to fund it. Earning capacity and living expenses have clearly to be weighed in the balance and the reduction programme based on the most pessimistic estimate. It is pointless to dream of reductions beyond the reach of the customer and the business relationship will be jeopardised when the borrower experiences difficulty in keeping up with his monthly payments. Each month the customer has to accumulate in his current account a reserve sufficient to meet the transfer to the loan on the agreed date. Does the finance budget prove beyond doubt that this can be achieved regularly without undue difficulty after full allowance for imponderables? This is surely the crucial test. It would be better not to lend at all if there is any doubt on this point.

All these features will be examined and the information collated during the course of the initial interview with the customer, who being in need of the financial support must be prepared to furnish the bank, in confidence, with a complete picture. If the information is disclosed frankly and efficiently, the banker will be impressed with the financial acumen of the customer, but any halting approach or attempt to forget current commitments will destroy confidence. The applicant for a personal loan needs the money to satisfy his requirements and has to be prepared to reveal his complete financial position. The banker, on the other side of the desk, is contemplating an unsecured advance and cannot therefore, hold his punches, but must indulge in plain speaking and frank advice. Here is the opportunity to display the judgment and skill as a lender which has been discussed throughout this volume. The daily work of most managers has undoubtedly increased, but they have welcomed this revival of real lending to personal customers for private requirements. The success of their efforts depends upon the size of the bad debts incurred in relation to the total amount lent by them within the personal loans scheme. A personal loan is indeed the surest test of sound lending and the basic principles have to applied to every proposal, otherwise blind lending on snap judgments will end in bad debts.

CONSUMER CREDIT LEGISLATION

In most developed countries and particularly in western Europe and North America, Government legislation has been introduced to modify the affects of the old adage "caveat emptor"–buyer beware. High pressure promotion, dubious selling techniques and complex loan agreement forms have been used by unscrupulous concerns to encourage consumers to spend and borrow beyond their means. In societies where employment is protected to a large degree by the State and unemployment pay is sufficiently high to cover reasonable living standards the certainty of repayment of personal financial commitments, within limits, is virtually guaranteed. The exploitation of the consumer by the supplier of goods and the lender of money has, therefore, been judged as an area requiring direct intervention by the State.

Inan attempt to draw up rules and regulations to define fair practices in the provision of loans to meet consumer purchases the legislators have been unable to devise procedures to restrict the operations of the small minority of the financial community who trade integrity for profit without penalising the majority with time consuming, expensive bureaucratic systems for providing personal advances.

CONSUMER CREDIT ACT 1974

Although the Consumer Credit Act received the Royal Assent on 31st July, 1974 only the first two parts of the Act came into force on that day providing definitions of the Government's power in this field and the terms used in the legislation. Subsequently, a third part providing that all consumer credit grantors should be licensed by the Director General of Fair Trading instituted the first measure of overall Government control on the credit industry in terms of consumer protection. All the remaining ten parts are being implemented by stages through the issue of statutory regulations from time to time. The animated debate which took place between politicians, civil servants and interested parties, including those representing the banks and consumer interests spread over two years while the original bills passed through the House of Commons. The same process of consultation and argument continues as the law is translated into administrative effect.

The following sections cover the main features of this highly complex piece of legislation as seen during this transitional phase. This summary, which would require far more detail to be comprehensive is intended to give the reader a view of the situation when the whole Act is implemented. Indications are given where the implications of the new regulations are not yet entirely clear.

CONSUMER CREDIT AGREEMENTS

The basic numeraire of the Act is the credit agreement whereby a creditor provides a debtor with credit of any amount; a consumer credit agreement is a contract for any form of loan to an "individual", as defined by the Act, not exceeding £5,000. Advances of £5,000 or less for house purchase remain consumer credit agreements but are generally exempted from the provisions of the Act.

Various forms of consumer credit agreement are defined in the legislation. These forms can be considered, for the purposes of the lending banker, under two main headings—running account credit, where the lending is provided on a continuous in and out basis subject to an overall limit and fixed-sum credit where the advance is taken on more formalised terms either by one amount or by instalments. This division exemplified by the overdraft and personal loan facilities respectively are subject to different treatment under the Act as will be seen in the following paragraphs.

Two types of consumer credit agreement are also of relevance:
- (i) agreements where a credit token is involved—a card, voucher, coupon, form or other document which enables the borrower to obtain cash, goods or services on credit;
- (ii) agreements where the credit is provided specifically to finance purchases from a particular supplier.

Special provisions are contained in the Act as regards these types of agreements. For example, that it is an offence to provide a person with a credit token if he has not asked for it; that is to say, direct mailing of credit cards would create an offence under the legislation. Again, if the agreement restricts the provision of credit to purchases from one source of supply the creditor becomes jointly and severally liable with the supplier for claims for misrepresentation or breach of contract by the debtor; thus the banker becomes involved in obligations of warranty as regards the goods of the supplier and this refers, for example, to individual store credit card schemes administered by banks or general use credit cards accepted in retail stores.

In due course, consumer credit agreements covered by the Act will not be legally executed unless the agreements are expressed in legible writing in documents in the prescribed form containing all the minimum terms laid down by the Secretary of State. At some stage, therefore, all facilities under £5,000 provided by the bank to a non-corporate customer will need to be evidenced by written agreements containing, *inter alia*, the rights and duties conferred or imposed by the agreement on the borrower, his protection and remedies under the Act and the amount and rate of the total charge for credit to be levied by the lender. This requirement necessarily raises the question of the informal or unsanctioned overdraft on current account, where the customer takes credit, often without prior arrangement with his banker or of an amount which exceeds that arrangement. An exclusion is provided in the Act at the discretion of the Director General of Fair Trading as far as written documentation is concerned for overdrafts in general. From a practical banker's viewpoint it is clear the present personal overdraft service provided by the clearing banks could not survive should this exclusion prove to be illusory.

ENTRY INTO CONSUMER CREDIT AGREEMENTS

Regulations will be issued in due course covering the completion of credit agreements between lenders and borrowers. These regulations will specify the minimum information which will need to be given to the borrower before completion, the minimum contents of the final documentation and how copies of this documentation are to be made available to the borrower before and after completion by both parties.

Minimum requirements are also laid down in the Act regarding access to information by the debtor during the course of the loan. These requirements are well within the present practices of all clearing banks, but give an indication of the basic intention of the Act which is to protect unwary borrowers from the sharp practices of the fringe credit operator.

The terms and methods which may be used by a lender to serve notice of default on the debtor and thereafter terminate the agreement are given in Part VII of the Act. While these provisions concern primarily hire purchase and the hire of consumer goods, the banker may be affected by the minimum requirements for information and rebate of charges in the event of the early repayment of a loan.

Finally, the Act specifies in Part VIII the processes to be used in taking security for a loan. These sections cover the form and content of written forms of charge, the lender's duties towards the borrower and towards any surety as regards information and documentation and the regulation of realisation of security if this should prove necessary.

CANCELLATION OF THE AGREEMENT

The most important feature of any lending facility for both the borrower and the lender is for the parties concerned to be confident that final agreement has been reached so that the money may be drawn and used without undue delay. In order to protect the unwary or impetuous borrower from financial commitments beyond his capacity to repay, special provisions have been incorporated in the Act to allow subsequent cancellation of the credit agreement by the borrower within what is called euphemistically the cooling-off period. This facility to withdraw from a consumer credit agreement becomes operative if the preliminary negotiations included oral representation in the presence of the prospective borrower. If such was the case cancellation may take place up to five days after the debtor has received the final documentation for the agreement or up to 14 days after his signing the agreement itself. Special care has to be taken where the consumer credit agreement is secured by a land mortgage. In this case the borrower has to be provided with the unexecuted documentation prior to completion and given a minimum of seven days to "consider" the agreement. Fortunately, this does not apply to bridging loans.

For the banker the exclusions for this cancellation provision are important. First of all it is anticipated that agreements concerning overdrafts on current account are exempted and secondly where formalised personal lending facilities are being arranged, signature of the documentation by the debtor on bank premises constitutes a binding contract for the purposes of this Act.

Even when the contract between lender and borrower is completed and the money lent the Court reserves the right to reopen consideration of an agreement of any size where a question of extortion is raised—one presumes by the debtor. Usury appears to be defined in relation to current economic conditions, certainly the interest rates charged in these inflationary times would have shocked our judges of years gone by. The Court's considerations of exorbitant will range beyond interest rates to all the terms of the agreement and one can applaud the purpose of this wide power. Although the clearing banker can safely ignore such conditions as highly unlikely to affect his services, unwarranted litigation can cause considerable nuisance and expense.

Perhaps some of the most interesting and perplexing aspects of this legislation relate to the antecedent negotiations referred to in determining the application of the cancellation provisions. It is an offence under the Act to canvass a consumer credit agreement away from the bank's own premises. Again, amongst other exemptions bank overdrafts for an existing customer are excluded from these provisions at the discretion of the Director General of Fair Trading, but in general terms a banker cannot agree a personal loan facility with an individual away from his own office buildings. The banker can avoid such an offence, which could involve him in personal liability, by refusing to commit himself formally unless the borrower visits his branch or by completing the arrangement in writing or by receiving a written request from his customer to visit him to discuss a lending proposition. These rules should be respected, particularly as regards lending to minors where in addition sending literature advertising bank advances constitutes an offence. A practical banker would probably wish to avoid such loans in any case, but care should be taken when addressing schools or other educational establishments to avoid mentioning lending services when explaining the advantages of a banking account to young people.

Marketing the banks' services is an essential part of any branch banker's everyday duties and in letters, leaflets and booklets quotations will be given for specific or general lending arrangements. In all such cases, whether for overdraft or any other form of lending service, the total charge for the credit including all forms of interest, plus any ancillary or connected commission charge must be given in writing in a prescribed form. This aspect relates particularly to all forms of advertising where personal credit is involved.

It is often useful to consider the bringing together of a number of services to be sold to an individual or groups of individuals. Sometimes it is possible to arrange special discounts on some facilities when linked together with other services. In these instances the total charge for credit provisions apply to the overall "package". As regards any advertisement for a personal credit facility, which is available for sums under £5,000, the form and content must convey a fair and reasonably comprehensive indication of the nature of the facility. Where the credit offered is restricted to the purchase of particular goods or to goods provided by a particular supplier, the purchaser must be offered cash terms as an alternative.

The cancellation provisions of the Act may seem to be of concern primarily to those devising the marketing policies and implementing new services for the commercial banks. Nevertheless, for the practical banker in his everyday duties care must be taken in his normal social intercourse within his community to avoid contravening the canvassing provisions. In writing letters to his customers, when lecturing to schools, remitting credit cards or completing the documentation on a personal loan, the provisions of the Act must remain fresh in his mind. Failure to do so could involve a technical offence against the present law or subsequent cancellation of a debt with the attendant cost of obtaining repayment of the funds lent.

Index

Assets	Cost	Deprecia-tion		M/V
	£	£	£	
Goodwill	5,000	—	5,000	
FIXED ASSETS				
(F) Factory and Land	16,000	4,000	12,000	
Plant and Machinery	12,000	3,000	9,000	
Fixtures and Fittings .	4,500	1,500	3,000	
Motors . . .	6,000	2,000	4,000	
	43,500	10,500	33,000	
Quoted Investments, at cost (market value 30/4/78 £4,250)			4,000	
Trade Investments at cost .		2,800		
Trade Investments at cost .		800		
Less amount written off. .		—	2,000	
FLOATING ASSETS				
Stock in hand (as valued by directors)		16,000		
Work-in-Progress . . .		8,000		
			24,000	
Debtors		28,000		
Less Reserve for Bad and Doubtful Debts		2,000		
			26,000	
Cash in Hand			1,000	
			90,000	

he best of our knowledge and belief were necessary for the purposes
kept by the Company so far as appears from our examination of
eement with the books of account and returns. In our opinion and
given us, the said Balance Sheet gives the information required by
d, with the foregoing observation, gives a true and fair view of the

(Signed) ....

(Date) ....